A Journey to Less:
A Life Designed for More

A Journey to Less:
A Life Designed for More

Clear the clutter, embrace simplicity, and uncover the joy of living with less

Rita Wilkins "The Downsizing Designer"

DESIGN SERVICES, LTD
4023 Kennett Pike Suite 274
Greenville DE, 19807

Copyright© 2025 Design Services LTD
All rights reserved. No portion of this book may be duplicated, reproduced, or distributed without written permission from the author. This book may not be stored in a system maintained for retrieval of materials or transmitted in any electronic or digital form such as photocopying, scanning, photographing, and recording.

To request permission to use this material email
ritawilkins@ritawilkins.com

Quotations and attributions used in publications, articles, book reviews, and websites do not require written permission from the author.

First Edition: February 2025
ISBN (paperback): 978-1-7334338-2-2

Contact information: ritawilkins@ritawilkins.com.
Website: www.designservicesltd.com.

Designed by Elene Tierra

Acknowledgment from the Author
I want to acknowledge and extend my sincerest appreciation to Elene Tierra, my extremely talented project and marketing-manager, for her creativity, profound insights, and dedication to helping me compile, organize, and produce our new e-book, *A Journey to Less: A Life Designed for More*.

I would also like to thank Guy Edwards of Brainjar Media, my SEO guru and marketing specialist, for his valuable input and keen insights, drawn from his many years of experience.

This book came to life because of our team's dedication and commitment to helping our global audience experience the joy of living a more abundant life with less.

CONTENTS

INTRODUCTION		**1**
CHAPTER 1	**Introduction to Minimalism and Decluttering**	**3**
	1. The Gift That Changed My Life (It Could Change Yours Too!)	4
	2. Lifestyle Trends: Why Baby Boomers Are Embracing Minimalism	10
	3. Therapeutic Benefits of Decluttering Your Home and Your Life	17
	4. The Hidden Life-Changing Power of Decluttering	23
CHAPTER 2	**Practical Steps for Decluttering**	**29**
	1. Are You "Dueling" with Clutter? How to Win the Battle and Get Your Life Back	30
	2. Decluttering? 10 Easy Steps to Get Started and Stay Motivated	37
	3. The Truth About Downsizing and Decluttering: What No One Tells You, But Your Need to Know	46
	4. Get Your Own House Back! Stop Being a Repository for Other People's Stuff	53
	5. How a Reverse Bucket List Can Reboot and Reignite Your Life and Career	59
CHAPTER 3	**Emotional and Legacy Considerations**	**67**
	1. Mom, Thanks but No Thanks: The Rebellion Against Family Heirlooms	68
	2. It's Just Grandma's Old Stuff Until It's Vintage— Then It's Chic	75

	3. What Do You Do When You Want to Downsize—But Your Spouse Doesn't?	81
	4. Leave a Lasting Legacy: It's What We Do, Not What We Have	87
	5. Dare to Dream Again After Being Hit by a Life Quake	96
CHAPTER 4	**Lifestyle Design—Minimalist's Mindset**	**100**
	1. 5 Top Secrets to Beat Decision Fatigue with Fewer Choices	101
	2. Make Yourself at Home in Your Own Home	108
	3. Living Small but Having It All	113
	4. A Comprehensive Guide to House Sharing: Make Your Home Roommate Ready	118
	5. Silver Learnings: How COVID-19 Turned Out to Be the Best Thing That Happened to Me	123
CHAPTER 5	**Adventure and Financial Freedom—Freedom Through Minimalism**	**127**
	1. Bring Back the Adventure, Freedom, and Fun That's Been Missing From Your Life	126
	2. 10 Lessons That Come From Living Outside of Your Comfort Zone	135
	3. Stop Wasting Money: Five Effective Strategies to Reduce the Temptation to Overbuy Online	144
	4. Why Teaching Grandkids About Money Early Matters	149
	5. Downsized? How to Decorate Your New Smaller Home for the Holidays	157

Supplementary Materials	**163**
Decluttering Checklist	**164**
The Reverse Bucket List	**165**
Bonus Article: Life Audit Article	**173**

INTRODUCTION

Hello, and welcome to a journey that has changed my life—and I hope will change yours, too.

I'm Rita Wilkins, also known as "The Downsizing Designer," and I've dedicated my life to helping others embrace the transformative power of living with less. Over the years, I've shared my experiences through writing, speaking, and working with people who, like you, are searching for clarity, peace, and purpose in their lives.

This eBook is deeply personal to me. It's more than just a guide—it's a compilation of articles I've written over the past several years, woven together with stories, insights, and practical strategies that have helped countless people break free from clutter and reclaim their lives.

Through these pages, I'll take you on a journey into the heart of minimalism. You'll read about the therapeutic benefits of decluttering and why so many of us are overwhelmed by "stuff." You'll discover practical steps to tackle even the most daunting piles of clutter and learn how to navigate the emotional challenges of letting go—whether it's sentimental heirlooms, relationship baggage, or even outdated dreams.

But this journey is about more than just physical spaces. It's about rethinking our choices, our priorities, and how we want to spend the precious time we have. You'll find inspiration to live more intentionally, design a home and life that truly reflect who you are, and rediscover the joy and freedom that come from living with less.

Rita Wilkins, "The Downsizing Designer"

I've poured my heart into this eBook because I believe in the life-changing power of simplicity. By the end, I hope you'll feel empowered, inspired, and ready to take the first step—or the next step—on your own journey to a simpler, more fulfilling life.

Let's begin together. There's so much waiting for you on the other side of less.

Rita S. Wilkins

— Rita Wilkins, "The Downsizing Designer"

WATCH ON YOUTUBE:

CHAPTER 1

Introduction to Minimalism and Decluttering

How we choose to spend our time, energy, and resources matters.

Let go of things that prevent you from living fully each day in accordance with what matters most to you.

ARTICLE 1

The Gift That Changed My Life… It Could Change Yours Too!

I was talking with a friend this morning who said,

> "I'm already exhausted… and the holiday season just began!"

She went on to say that she barely had time to enjoy Thanksgiving because she spent so much time and energy shopping, decorating, cooking, and cleaning that the actual dinner seemed like a big blur. At one point, she stated,

> "But the good news is, everyone else enjoyed it!"

As I listened, I was flooded with emotions and memories of my holidays past: I was her just a few years ago. I felt her pain and her desire to make everything perfect for everyone else, forgetting about her own wants and needs.

While excited to see the holidays come, I used to be even happier to see them go. Sad, but true.

THE GIFT OF TIME (THAT CHANGED MY LIFE)

Three years ago, I gave myself a gift that changed my life.

I gave myself **permission** to let go of having to do it all and to have it all be perfect. I gave myself the **freedom** to simply enjoy this special season—the lights, the sounds, and the smells.

Most of all, I gave myself the best gift I could ever give—the gift of more time to actually be with the people I love.

Introduction to Minimalism and Decluttering

THE SEASON OF BUYING

Black Friday is now over, but if we listen to the noisy marketing messages, "Tis the season to buy."

The hunt is on for the "perfect gifts" or the latest new gadgets. The mission is on to get the best holiday bargains for fear of missing out on things we "must have" to create the perfect holiday.

Think About the Numbers

According to the National Retail Federation:

- **114.6 Million Americans** were expected to shop on Black Friday.
- **174 Million people** were expected to shop between Thanksgiving and Cyber Monday.
- **$6.2 Billion dollars** were spent during that 5-day period.
- **65%** say they will shop **"because the deals are just too good to pass up."**

While those statistics are staggering, it is not just the number of people who will shop or the amount of money they will spend—it is the amount of precious time and energy that will NOT be spent with families and loved ones... time we can't get back.

What Will You Spend?

Before you decide to indulge in loads of holiday shopping, think about these questions:

1. Who or what is consuming your precious time this holiday season?
2. What is preventing you from slowing down and fully embracing the true meaning of the holidays?
3. What gift can you give yourself this year that will not only change your life but the lives of those you love the most?

Perhaps the best present of all is **you**. It could simply be your presence.

A FINAL THOUGHT

"If there is one thing I know for certain, it is that the most important things in life are not things at all. The memories created with those we love, conversations and laughter around the kitchen table, quality time spent with family, friends, and people in need, and a chance to make a difference in the world are the 'things' that bring the greatest joy."

Introduction to Minimalism and Decluttering

JOURNAL PROMPTS

- **Time and Presence:** What does the phrase "the gift of time" mean to you? How can you prioritize being present with loved ones this holiday season?
- **Holiday Perfectionism:** In what ways have you felt pressured to make the holidays "perfect"? How can you shift your focus to what truly matters?
- **Shopping Habits:** How do your shopping habits align with your values? Are there ways to make more meaningful gift-giving choices this year?

Quick Exercise
The Priorities List:

- Take 5 minutes to write down your top five priorities for the holiday season.
- Review the list and circle the ones that truly matter to your heart (e.g., spending quality time, creating joyful memories).
- For each circled item, write one small action you can take today to honor that priority.

Quick Tip
Pause Before You Purchase:

The next time you feel the urge to buy a holiday item, take a moment to ask yourself:

- Is this purchase adding joy or just clutter?
- Will this gift strengthen a connection or simply check a box?

Redirect your time and energy toward experiences or simple gestures that create lasting memories, like writing a heartfelt card or sharing a meaningful conversation.

Rita Wilkins, "The Downsizing Designer"

NOTES:

Introduction to Minimalism and Decluttering

*Who said we couldn't learn from our kids?
In many ways, they are far wiser than we were at an earlier age. Fortunately, we've learned that more stuff won't make us happy but more time, and energy spent on things that matter will.*

ARTICLE 2

Lifestyle Trend Goes Mainstream as Baby Boomers Embrace Minimalism

There's a cultural shift taking place right before our eyes. The generation that created consumerism is now embracing the idea of choosing to live with less… much less!

For years, baby boomers' big wallets and significant disposable income allowed them to buy big houses, fill them up with lots of beautiful stuff, then buy even bigger houses, and fill them up with even more stuff… and so it continued.

But as we've gotten older and a little wiser, and as we enter a new phase of our lives, many baby boomers are adopting minimalism as a lifestyle choice because they've discovered that less can really mean more.

- Less stuff, more freedom.
- More freedom, more life.
- Less clutter, simpler life.
- Simpler life, more happiness.

When you hear the word minimalism, you might naturally think of millennials, not baby boomers.

But a fast-growing trend within the baby boomer generation is to learn how to live abundantly with less… a lot less.

While the minimalist lifestyle spans across many generations, it is a relatively new concept to baby boomers, who, for years, adopted a consumer lifestyle of "bigger, better, more."

Introduction to Minimalism and Decluttering

We Have Learned

Many of us have learned a little bit about minimalism from our own adult children, who are extremely selective about what they allow into their homes and their lives. We may have even experienced a resounding "no" when we offered them some of our stuff as we decluttered our basements and attics.

Perhaps turned off by growing up in homes with an overabundance of stuff, the younger generations have clearly identified what they deem essential, and they also have the courage and willpower to say "no" to what's not necessary or useful.

Our generation is finally starting to realize that having excessive amounts of stuff not only creates clutter, disorder, and chaos in our homes and in our lives, but that stuff can also feel empty and meaningless. Many boomers have started to realize that when they intentionally remove the excess and unnecessary stuff, they free up time, money, and energy to focus on what matters most to them.

The days of spending so much of our time, money, and energy on accumulating "more" seems to be dissipating. Instead, we are beginning to discover what our kids knew all along: **LESS IS MORE!**

5 Key Factors Contributing to the Cultural Shift to Living with Less

1. **The Decluttering Movement**

    Marie Kondo's book and Netflix show, *Life-Changing Magic of Tidying Up: The Japanese Art of Decluttering and Organizing,* has had a major influence on people of all ages to live with less, and to embrace minimalism. In her book, Kondo encourages us to remove anything from our home that doesn't spark joy.

2. **The Pandemic**

   The Covid lockdown challenged baby boomers to rethink their priorities. Many were forced out of their jobs, while others opted for early retirement. In an effort to make their savings last longer, many baby boomers decided to declutter their large homes, downsize, and move to smaller homes to reduce expenses and live a simpler, more fulfilling life.

3. **Aging and Mortality**

   The pandemic also forced us to face our own mortality. Realizing that they were much happier not working, many baby boomers discovered new ways to live their best life right now while they still could. Many chose to sell their big homes and downsize so they could live closer to their children and grandchildren. They chose meaningful experiences with their family and loved ones over the big house and the big mortgage.

4. **Life Circumstances**

   When our lives change, so must we change and adapt. Divorce, death of a spouse, caregiving, and declining health are just a few situations we are faced with in our daily lives. Choosing to sell the family homestead, declutter, and downsize to a smaller, more affordable, and manageable home is often what's necessary to restore some semblance of calm in stressful, life-changing situations.

5. **Lifestyle Choice**

   Many boomers are just plain tired of the mental, physical, and financial burden of their once-beloved large homes and properties. They are ready to let go of much of the stuff that weighs them down and prevents them from living the life they really want: a lifestyle that provides more mobility, flexibility, and a lot less responsibility. They can then choose to spend their time

Introduction to Minimalism and Decluttering

on what matters most to them: their relationships, experiences, health, and passions that light them up.

We've Learned Much from Our Life Experiences

- ♦ More stuff doesn't make us happier.
- ♦ Too much stuff gets in the way of the more fulfilling life we could be living.
- ♦ Stuff is just stuff and it's no longer as important to us as it once was.

An overabundance of stuff causes clutter, and clutter comes with a cost to our health, well-being, and overall happiness —a cost, that at this stage of our lives, we cannot afford to pay.

Knowing that we have fewer years ahead of us than we do behind us, it's not at all surprising that we want to:

- ♦ MAXIMIZE our life experiences.
- ♦ MINIMIZE our excess clutter.

The trend towards minimalism—to travel light and pare down our possessions to only what we need, love, and use—is the natural off shoot of the wisdom gained from years of overindulging and overspending.

Settle for LESS

It's only natural that we want to settle for less in our third act—not less life, just less stuff so we can focus on what matters most.

The cultural shift and trend towards minimalism for boomers is an example of our shifting values as we age and how we are choosing to spend our time, money, energy, and resources.

At one point in our lives, we likely chose to buy more because it gave us pleasure, and we enjoyed it—the big house, the beautiful designer furniture, and the dinner table.

But at some point, perhaps not too long ago, we acknowledged that all of that stuff was just stuff

It felt empty. It felt superficial.

The never-ending desire for "more" robbed us of precious time and resources. The vicious cycle of buying "more" promised happiness but never really fulfilled on that promise.

As a baby boomer myself who has decluttered and downsized and now speaks nationally on the impact of living with less, I'm not at all surprised that baby boomers are embracing the freedom of less.

It's our third act, and by choosing to say goodbye to the emptiness of material possessions, we are saying hello to a richer, more abundant life.

We are going from a life full of stuff to a life filled with meaning.

Introduction to Minimalism and Decluttering

JOURNAL PROMPTS
- What is one area of your life where you feel weighed down by "stuff," and how would letting it go improve your happiness?

Quick Exercise
- Choose one drawer, shelf, or small space to declutter.
- Remove anything you no longer use or love. List item #3

Quick Tip
- Adopt the "one in, one out" rule: For every new item you bring into your home, donate or discard one you no longer need.

NOTES:
_____
_____
_____
_____
_____
_____
_____
_____
_____
_____
_____
_____
_____
_____
_____
_____

It can take over your home and your life. It can take a huge toll on your health, wealth, and happiness.

Decluttering, on the other hand, is the antidote to stress, overwhelmed, and lack of productivity, improve your mood, your sleep, and your peace of mind.

Introduction to Minimalism and Decluttering

ARTICLE 3

Therapeutic Benefits of Decluttering Your Home and Your Life

Clutter... We've all experienced it—some visible, some hidden. Physical and mental clutter have a funny way of creeping into our homes and our lives. Slowly but surely, we become inundated and overwhelmed by it, sometimes to the point of making us sick.

VISIBLE CLUTTER

Think Paper Clutter

Stacks of junk mail, takeout menus, bills, and advertisements accumulate on kitchen counters, desks, and coffee tables. When ignored, this clutter spreads like a virus, making it hard to focus or relax.

Think Digital Clutter

Unopened emails, messy desktops, and thousands of unorganized photos we promise to delete "someday" build up. Left unchecked, digital disarray disrupts productivity and adds unnecessary stress.

Think Sentimental Clutter

Photos, love letters, and keepsakes often pile up in boxes, tucked away in attics or basements. Though hidden, their presence weighs on us, reminding us of the emotional task of sorting through memories someday.

Think Calendar Clutter

Overbooked calendars filled with obligations we dread leave no room for personal priorities or downtime. Without "white space," we risk burnout and neglect our true desires.

HIDDEN CLUTTER

Think Relationship Clutter

Toxic relationships filled with yelling, shaming, or controlling behaviors clutter our emotional lives. Just like physical clutter, these relationships can hold us back from living fully.

Think Financial Clutter

Without a budget, overdue bills, impulse purchases, and maxed-out credit cards create invisible chaos, leading to stress and anxiety.

THE IMPACT OF CLUTTER

Whether visible or hidden, clutter takes a toll on our health, finances, and happiness. Like a disease, it slowly diminishes the quality of life.

Recognizing the hold clutter has on you is the first step toward freedom and discovering the therapeutic benefits of decluttering.]

COMMON EMOTIONAL ROADBLOCKS TO DECLUTTERING

1. Overwhelm

- ♦ **Problem:** The sheer size of the task feels unmanageable.
- ♦ **Solution:** Start small—one drawer or shelf at a time. Seeing progress motivates you to continue.

Introduction to Minimalism and Decluttering

2. Sentimentality
- **Problem:** Difficulty letting go of items tied to memories.
- **Solution:** Keep a few cherished items, take photos, and create albums. Document why those items are meaningful.

3. Procrastination
- **Problem:** Wanting to declutter but continually putting it off.
- **Solution:** Set a deadline and stick to a schedule. Ask a friend to help keep you accountable.

4. Fear
- **Problem:** Worry about discarding something you might need later.
- **Solution:** Develop a decluttering mindset. Over time, it becomes easier, and you'll enjoy the freedom of living with less.

5. Guilt
- **Problem:** Feeling guilty about letting go of expensive purchases or gifts.
- **Solution:** Accept that the money has been spent or that gifts are yours to keep—or not. Focus on the ease and simplicity of a clutter-free life.

Reframing Decluttering as a Positive Experience

Decluttering is emotional, but it doesn't have to be negative. Let yourself process feelings of fear, guilt, and attachment. Allow yourself to grieve the loss or donation of items.

When you shift your mindset, decluttering becomes about **what you gain**, not what you lose. It can restore clarity, peace of mind, and happiness.

Benefits of Decluttering

- Relieves stress and overwhelm.
- Creates physical and mental space.
- Simplifies your home and lifestyle.
- Improves focus, freedom, and peace of mind.

Decluttering isn't just about getting rid of excess. It's about creating boundaries and habits that prevent clutter from returning.

Introduction to Minimalism and Decluttering

JOURNAL PROMPTS
- What items in my home spark joy and which ones create stress?
- How would I feel if I let go of things I haven't used in over a year?
- What cluttered spaces in my home bother me the most, and why?
- How can I honor sentimental items without keeping all of them?

Quick Exercise
- **Five-Minute Sweep:** Set a timer for five minutes and tackle one cluttered area (e.g., a drawer, desktop, or corner). Stop when the timer goes off and repeat daily.

Quick Tip
For every new item you bring into your home, commit to letting go of at least one old item.

NOTES:
_____
_____
_____
_____
_____
_____
_____
_____
_____
_____
_____
_____

Rita Wilkins, "The Downsizing Designer"

This is a real-life story of a woman who not only got her home back after decluttering but also her life! That's the power of decluttering from the inside out.

ARTICLE 4

The Hidden Life-Changing Power of Decluttering

Who could have guessed that the cathartic process of purging and decluttering one woman's home—one drawer, one closet, one room at a time—could change the direction and trajectory of her life forever?

What began as an attempt to help a client gradually declutter her home, which had become so overrun with clutter that she was overwhelmed to the point of feeling paralyzed and powerless to accomplish the task on her own, turned into an unexpected adventure and great revelation.

What happened was completely unexpected. After almost a year of decluttering, a powerful, confident, and emboldened woman emerged from under all that clutter. The physical and emotional clutter that had been standing in the way of the peace, contentment, and fulfillment she now experiences in her clutter-free home was gone.

Even more importantly, after fully embracing the inner work of decluttering, she became a woman who loved and respected herself enough to confront anyone—including herself—who told her she couldn't, when she knew she *could*.

But perhaps the most significant impact of decluttering, both the physical and mental clutter, was the life-changing power that she discovered within herself, hidden underneath all of that stuff.

GETTING YOUR LIFE BACK THROUGH DECLUTTERING

Several major transformations took place during the nine-month-long process:

- ♦ She regained control of her physical environment by purging anything that she no longer wanted, needed, or used, creating space for a simpler and more abundant life with less.
- ♦ She reclaimed her own power by discovering a new sense of control over herself and her life, ultimately making room for the life she really wanted.
- ♦ She rediscovered her self-worth, self-love, inner peace, contentment, and happiness.

Throughout the process of purging, she also learned how to:

- ♦ Confront and talk about the deep-seated emotions of anger, resentment, and frustration that had been building up and kept hidden for many years.
- ♦ Reject and refuse to allow the negative, non-supportive environment that prevented her from accomplishing her decluttering goals. Instead, she replaced them with a supportive team that would inspire and encourage her on the journey.
- ♦ Develop new skills, routines, and habits that would contribute to sustainable changes.

"GOOD LUCK WITH THAT!"

A few weeks into our decluttering sessions, I was introduced to her spouse for the first time.

She said, "Rita is here to help me declutter our home."

He responded, "Good luck with that!"

Introduction to Minimalism and Decluttering

To this day, those cruel, biting, and disempowering words still ring in my ears!

In that moment, I saw a woman who had heard this message many times before and felt so beaten down by a spouse who was betting against her success.

How could she possibly win at decluttering—or anything else she set out to do? No wonder she felt incapable of doing this project on her own!

THOSE WERE "FIGHTING WORDS!"

His disrespectful words lit a fire and passion within me to not only help this woman get her house back but also to reclaim her power, self-respect, and belief in herself. I was committed to having her reverse the real-time cost of clutter.

Getting Started, Staying Motivated, and Winning the Decluttering Game

Here's an overview of the process of this life-changing approach to decluttering:

- ♦ Establish ground rules for a safe, supportive, and judgment-free space that inspires and encourages weekly progress.
- ♦ Teach practical tools, tips, and techniques to let go of excess that is not aligned with values and current lifestyle.
- ♦ Practice techniques for overcoming obstacles and breaking free of barriers that slow down the decision-making process.
- ♦ Take "before pictures" and "after pictures" at every decluttering session.
- ♦ Complete the initial intake form/questionnaire to better understand the impact of physical and emotional clutter on health, well-being, relationships, productivity, and overall happiness.

- ♦ Monitor the level of weekly commitment and keep a written journal.
- ♦ Create a written vision statement for life after decluttering.
- ♦ Create a blueprint/roadmap of all areas in the home to be decluttered. Prioritize them in order of importance and impact.
- ♦ Establish a decluttering calendar with specific dates, times, and goals for each session.
- ♦ Document weekly progress, noting whether goals were achieved. If not, why not? What might be done differently the next time: lessons learned.

Room by Room, Session by Session, We Began to See Real Transformation and Results

As she grew to trust me, she openly talked about the emotions that she had been denying and attempting to hide for many years. Those feelings of anger, resentment, frustration, and disrespect began to melt away, and feelings of gratitude and hope started to creep into our conversations.

She came to realize that, as she had lost control of her house and the clutter within it, she had also lost her own power and self-respect.

With each bag of discarded trash, with each box of donated items, she wasn't just letting go of physical clutter; she was also letting go of the mental clutter that had been the real roadblock to any possibility of success.

As her house started to feel lighter, brighter, and more organized, she too began to exude a newfound power, self-confidence, and self-respect.

During the nine-month-long journey of decluttering and of getting her house and her life back, she discovered the real cost of clutter. The woman who had been hiding beneath it all began to emerge.

Introduction to Minimalism and Decluttering

A Good Ending

We all like good endings, and this one will warm your heart. About six months into the process, her spouse began to compliment her on her commitment and progress. He even offered to help.

A month before we finished the large project, her husband happily announced that they had decided to have a big party at their house—something they both were too ashamed to do in the past.

At last, together, they could proudly invite people into their new home. Success!

Rita Wilkins, "The Downsizing Designer"

JOURNAL PROMPTS

- ♦ What is one item in your home that no longer serves you? What emotions are tied to it?
- ♦ How do you envision your ideal home? Describe it in detail, including the feelings it evokes.
- ♦ What's one area of your home that you feel most overwhelmed by? What steps could you take to start clearing it?

Quick Exercise

- ♦ **The One-Shelf Test:** Start with a small, manageable area like a shelf or drawer. Clear it out completely. Reflect on how it feels to have a tidy, clutter-free space.

Quick Tips

- ♦ Start small and focus on one room or area at a time.
- ♦ Take photos before and after each session to see your progress.
- ♦ Keep a "donate" box in a visible place and add one item a day. Drop it off weekly at a local charity.
- ♦ Set a timer for 20 minutes and declutter for that short burst of time. It's often easier to get started when the task seems less daunting.

NOTES:
_____
_____
_____
_____
_____

CHAPTER II

Practical Steps for Decluttering

*How do you know when you won
the battle over clutter?*

*When you look around and say, I have all I want,
all I need, I have enough. I am enough!*

ARTICLE 1

Are You "Dueling" with Clutter? How to Win the Battle and Get Your Life Back

Are You Fighting a Never-Ending Battle with Clutter?

If you think you are alone, you're not!

According to the National Association of Professional Organizers:

- ♦ 54% of Americans are overwhelmed by clutter.
- ♦ 55% say clutter is a huge source of stress.
- ♦ 33% hold onto things they no longer want, need, or use.

Americans are "dueling" with too much stuff, and they know it is impacting their health, wealth, and relationships. It is costing them time, money, energy—and focus.

THE PAIN OF LIVING CLUTTERED LIVES

The other day, I received a call from a new client, who was responding to an article I had written, *Breaking Up with Your Stuff Is Hard to Do*.

She said:

> "I really need your help. I can't seem to get rid of all the clutter in my home. It is everywhere and it is literally making me sick! I'm overwhelmed and don't know where to start. No matter how many new storage containers and organizers I buy, my problem just seems to get worse."

STOP!

Practical Steps for Decluttering

Buying more pretty baskets, storage containers, or organizing bins is like putting a band-aid on a gaping wound.

Americans are drowning in their stuff, and we are making desperate attempts (like buying more files, shelves, and plastic bins) to try to take back control of our lives. Our overabundance of "stuff" is making us miserable, causing stress, anxiety, frustration, overwhelm, and embarrassment.

The impact that it has on the quality of our lives is immense. Our cluttered lives prevent us from living a simpler life with less so we have more time, money, freedom, and energy to pursue what matters most to us.

In my TEDx Talk, *Downsize Your Life: Why Less is More*, I confess to once owning 11 closets and 9 rolling racks of clothes. My ultimate realization during my downsizing and decluttering journey was that buying more "stuff" didn't make me happier.

In fact, the more I bought, the emptier and less fulfilled I became. Once I disrupted the downward spiral of thinking I needed more, and once I changed my relationship to "stuff," I won the battle! Stuff no longer owned or consumed my life. I got my life back and never looked back!

Is There a Clutter Crisis in America?

Americans are drowning in "stuff," yet we continue to buy more. Let me o er a few scary clutter statistics:

- ◆ 300,000—This is the average number of items in the American home (UCLA study: A Cluttered Life).
- ◆ 11%—Americans who rented a storage unit in 2020 at a cost of $1,095 per year (Bloomberg).
- ◆ $38 billion—The value of the storage industry in 2018, with more than 50,000 facilities in the U.S. (Bloomberg).

Rita Wilkins, "The Downsizing Designer"

Is It Time to Let Go of Your Stuff and Get Your Life Back?

Every day, people ask me to help them solve their own clutter crisis. But before dealing with the physical clutter, it's even more important to honestly address these difficult and confronting questions:

WHY Do You Want to Declutter?

- What is the impact clutter is having on the quality of your life and on your happiness?
- What is it costing you in time, money, energy, and freedom?
- How is it impacting your relationships?

WHY Do You Buy and Accumulate More Than You Need?

Does it...

- Make you feel more secure?
- Make you feel happier and less lonely after loss or divorce?
- Make you feel more important or more successful?
- Help you feel like you can measure up to others?

WHY Do You Have Difficulty Letting Go of Stuff?

We often attach meaning to our stuff and are afraid, resist, or procrastinate in letting go:

- **Sentiment**—Our "stuff" can be reminders or memories of special people, places, or times in our lives.
- **Security**—Feeling safe and secure is a basic human need. Does owning an excessive amount of physical possessions make us feel safer and more secure?
- **Scarcity**—Fear of not having enough or being without can have us hold on tight. The idea that we spent "good money"

Practical Steps for Decluttering

on something and would be wasting it if we got rid of it is also a reason we don't want to let go.

♦ **Someday**—Resisting or procrastinating in letting go… just in case you might need it someday!

10-Step Plan to Win the Battle with Clutter

Here is a handy 10-step plan that can help you win your space for yourself and effectively get rid of clutter:

1. VISION

Create a vision for what your life will look like without clutter. Then, focus on what matters most in your life.

2. WILLINGNESS TO DO WHAT IT TAKES

Commit to making changes—getting rid of clutter and not allowing it back into your home and your life.

3. STOP BUYING MORE

Develop the mindset of having enough and being enough. You don't really need more.

4. CREATE A PLAN

Strategize. Set Goals. Create a Timeline. Track progress. Have accountability partners.

5. ASK FOR HELP

If you think you need help, ask for it. From family, friends, or professionals who are not emotionally attached to your stuff.

6. SCHEDULE DECLUTTERING

Pick a favorite decluttering method and a schedule that works for you and stick to it. Start small or start big. Just start today!

7. DEVELOP YOUR "LETTING GO" MUSCLE

If you don't want it, need it, or use it, let it go. Sell it, donate it, or repurpose it.

8. HAVE FUN

Make decluttering a game. Laugh at yourself and why you accumulated so much in the first place.

9. BE RESILIENT

You will get stuck, you will want to quit, you will question why you are doing this. Recall your reasons for wanting to live with less. This will serve as a reminder and motivate you to continue on your journey.

10. REMEMBER, THIS IS A JOURNEY

Along the way, you might actually realize how much less you need, but even better, how much less you want.

Decluttering is a process that takes time, effort, and commitment. It takes real courage to "duel" with your clutter. But, I assure you, it is a fight worth winning!

Practical Steps for Decluttering

JOURNAL PROMPTS

What is the most stressful area in your home right now? Why does it overwhelm you?

How does the clutter in your life affect your emotions and your ability to focus on what matters?

Quick Exercise

Clutter Audit: Walk through your home and note the areas where clutter accumulates most. Set a timer for 10 minutes, pick one area, and declutter as much as possible in that time. Reflect on how you feel afterward.

Quick Tip

Start with one small area—a drawer or countertop. The key to winning the clutter battle is taking it step by step.

NOTES:

_____
_____
_____
_____
_____
_____
_____
_____
_____
_____
_____
_____
_____

Rita Wilkins, "The Downsizing Designer"

No one said that decluttering would be easy, but what you may not have expected was the emotional roller coaster that you were about to embark on.

There were no warning signs that alerted you.

They just happened...
The tears, the overwhelm, then the resistance, and procrastination.

Practical Steps for Decluttering

ARTICLE 2

Decluttering? 10 Easy Steps to Get Started and Stay Motivated

Do you know the #1 challenge people face when decluttering their home? Getting started. And the #2 challenge? Staying motivated.

Congratulations if you've found the courage to take those first steps to declutter your home so that:

- ♦ Your kids won't have to clean out your home when you're gone.
- ♦ You can prepare for a fresh start when you retire.
- ♦ You can finally enjoy a simpler life with less stuff and less clutter.

THINK OF IT THIS WAY

You were successful at starting your decluttering journey because you took the time to:

- ♦ Create a vision for the life you want after decluttering.
- ♦ Develop a decluttering plan and timeline to accomplish your goals.
- ♦ Begin seeing the fruits of your efforts in the areas you've decluttered.

You were on a roll! WERE on a roll... past tense.

Losing Motivation

What happened to your drive to declutter once and for all? Why are you suddenly resisting, procrastinating, and finding every excuse not to dedicate time to decluttering?

You may not have anticipated the roadblocks, loss of momentum, and bouts of self-doubt. Despite previous efforts, the task ahead feels overwhelming again. Even the best-laid plans for a clutter-free home now seem like a distant dream.

THE MESSY MIDDLE

If this resonates, know you're not alone. The "messy middle" is where the going gets tough.

We're human. We lose excitement and enthusiasm to reach the finish line. We stop telling ourselves, "I can," and instead, we tell ourselves, "I can't. It's too hard." Then, we quit.

This mind game applies to many areas in life—losing weight, learning a new skill, or training for a marathon. It's not unusual to take one step forward and two steps back. So how do you pick yourself up and start over?

GETTING STUCK HAPPENS TO ALL OF US

Theodore Roosevelt once said, "If you believe you can, you're halfway there."

The first step is believing you can succeed. If you're committed to your decluttering goals and want to reignite your drive, follow these 10 simple steps.

10 SIMPLE STEPS TO GET STARTED AND STAY MOTIVATED ON YOUR DECLUTTERING JOURNEY

1. Deeply Connect with Why You Want to Declutter

What is your core reason for decluttering? This reason should resonate deeply with you.

Practical Steps for Decluttering

EXAMPLES:
- You don't want to leave your kids with the emotional burden of cleaning out your belongings.
- You dream of a "lighter" lifestyle in retirement, with freedom and flexibility.

2. Recommit to Your Vision for Life After Decluttering

Create a vision board that vividly depicts your clutter-free life. Place it somewhere visible to inspire you daily.

EXAMPLES:
- More time and energy to pursue adventures with loved ones.
- Weekly play dates with grandchildren while they're still young.

3. Acknowledge You Got Off Track

Admit that you've lost momentum and identify contributing factors.

EXAMPLES:
- Emotional impact of decluttering family photos.
- Physical exhaustion from doing it alone.
- Negative feedback from family or friends.

4. Celebrate Your Wins—Big and Small

Recognize your progress, even if it feels small. Recall what worked before to reignite your motivation.

EXAMPLE:
- Did the "burst method" of decluttering for 15-30 minutes daily help?

5. Identify When You Started to Lose Interest

Pinpoint the moments or triggers that caused you to lose focus.

EXAMPLES:
- **Naysayers:** People who discouraged you.
- **Emotional Triggers:** Items tied to strong memories.
- **Distractions:** Social media or phone calls stealing your time.

6. Have a Step-By-Step Plan for Overcoming Setbacks

Prepare a plan to navigate obstacles:
- Review your vision board daily.
- Declutter small, high-impact areas first.
- Alternate methods (burst, category, or room-by-room).
- Track progress with "before" and "after" photos.

7. Reframe Your Thinking from "Can't" to "Can"

Identify and counter negative self-talk. Replace "I can't" with positive affirmations.

TIPS:
- Smack down negative thoughts like "Whack-A-Mole."
- Be patient; over time, this habit will strengthen.

8. Surround Yourself with Supportive People

Engage accountability partners who celebrate your wins and encourage you during setbacks.

Practical Steps for Decluttering

9. Stay in the Moment

Focus on one task at a time. Completing small tasks builds momentum.

10. Have Fun While Decluttering

Discover ways to enjoy the process.

EXAMPLES:

- Host a decluttering party with friends. Work together, then share a meal and stories.
- Play music, listen to audiobooks, or enjoy podcasts as you work.

Don't Give Up

If you've lost motivation to declutter, don't give up. Believe in yourself and remember: *You're halfway there!*

As challenging as this journey may be, you'll learn so much about yourself. When you look back, you'll realize it was worth every minute.

Rita Wilkins, "The Downsizing Designer"

JOURNAL PROMPTS

- ♦ Write about the most meaningful reason you want to declutter. How would your life change if you lived with less?
- ♦ What types of items or areas are hardest for you to declutter? Why do you think that is?
- ♦ Imagine your decluttered home. How does it look, feel, and function? Write a detailed description to inspire yourself.

Quick Exercise

- ♦ Set a timer for 10 minutes and declutter a single area (like a drawer or shelf) as quickly as possible. Focus on progress, not perfection!
- ♦ Take a picture of a cluttered space before you start. Declutter for 15 minutes, then take an "after" picture.
- ♦ Compare the two to boost your motivation.

Quick Tips

- ♦ **The One-In, Two-Out Rule:** For every new item you bring into your home, remove two. This keeps clutter from creeping back in!
- ♦ **Create a Decluttering Playlist:** Curate an upbeat playlist or find a podcast that energizes you to keep decluttering fun and engaging.
- ♦ **Set Up a Donation Box:** Keep a box in a central location where you can easily drop items to donate. Once it's full, take it to your local charity!

Practical Steps for Decluttering

NOTES:

Rita Wilkins, "The Downsizing Designer"

*We all have a story to tell.
Share yours so we can learn from your experiences.*

Practical Steps for Decluttering

ARTICLE 3

The Truth About Downsizing and Decluttering: What No One Tells You, but You Need to Know

When I look back on my own downsizing journey, there are so many things I didn't know that I wish I had known at the time.

While I did get really good at figuring things out over time, it sure would have made the process a lot easier had I known then what I know now—the truth about downsizing and decluttering, what no one tells you but what you need to know.

With the ever-increasing popularity of downsizing and decluttering across all ages and demographics, it's important for you to know what to expect before you embark on this life-changing decision.

So, if you are considering a decluttering and downsizing journey and want to know the good, the bad, and the ugly about the process so you can be better informed, please read till the end of my blog to learn from my successes as well as my mistakes.

THE GOOD: The Surprising Benefits of Decluttering and Downsizing My Life

After decluttering and downsizing, one of the biggest surprises was how simple my life had become.

Having broken free of the burden of clutter and a home filled with too much stuff, my smaller environment was organized and peaceful, and I knew where everything was. I was no longer wasting time looking for things.

Living in a smaller home with much less stuff suddenly just made sense! I had more time, money, freedom, and energy to do all the things I had been wanting to do. I could now focus on what mattered to me because nothing was holding me back. I was in control of my own life. I had all I wanted, all I needed, and I had never been happier.

I also realized how little I actually needed and how the quality of my life had improved. My only question was: Why hadn't I decluttered and downsized sooner?

THE BAD: The Daily Challenges You Face During the Downsizing and Decluttering Journey

Note that these so-called challenges also became opportunities each day to learn, grow, and become stronger in my resolve to simplify my life.

THE EMOTIONAL ROLLER COASTER:
Uncertainty and Fear of the Unknown

Each day seemed to bring on a new emotion:

- ♦ Overwhelm, stress, peace
- ♦ Tears, sadness, joy
- ♦ Indecisiveness, decisiveness, clarity

At any given moment, I was filled with self-doubt:

- ♦ What if I need it someday?
- ♦ How can I possibly let go of my sentimental items?
- ♦ What do I need to do to stay motivated when I want to give up?
- ♦ Is it worth all this time and effort?

Acknowledging these complex emotions is critical to your decluttering and downsizing success. They're perfectly normal. Anyone who declutters and downsizes experiences many similar emotions.

Practical Steps for Decluttering

The key to success is not to dwell on the emotions and things that hold you back. Instead, constantly remind yourself of WHY you want to downsize and declutter.

Whether it's to save money, live a simpler life, or have more freedom, shift your focus to one small area, like a drawer, and make one small decision at a time.

This mindset shift is magical because it will help you get unstuck so you can move forward.

THE UGLY: What NOT to Do When Downsizing and Decluttering

Here are 5 big mistakes I made during my journey to owning less. Avoiding these can save you a lot of time, trouble, and heartache:

1. **Trying to do it all at once.** This is not only impossible but also unwise. Take the time upfront to create a plan and implement your project one area at a time. Set realistic goals, timelines, and intentions for where you'll live and where your excess items will go.

2. **Trying to do it alone.** After one exhausting month of decluttering solo, I realized I needed a team. Having support allowed me to create a workable plan and even enjoy the process.

3. **Bringing too much stuff to your smaller** home. Overpacking a smaller space is a common mistake. Be mindful of the limited storage in your new home and make thoughtful decisions about what to bring.

4. **Waiting too long to downsize and declutter.** I delayed my move by five years, which led to unnecessary stress, wasted resources, and missed opportunities for joy. Living with less has added years to the quality of my life.

5. **Continuing to accumulate more.** Breaking the cycle of over-accumulation is essential. Learning to say no and understanding your relationship with "more" is critical for living a simpler, more meaningful life.

MISCONCEPTIONS ABOUT DECLUTTERING AND DOWNSIZING

"Downsizing is stressful and overwhelming."

While there's an element of stress, with the right mindset and tools, the process can be smooth, enjoyable, and even fun.

"Decluttering and downsizing means sacrificing comfort."

This is not true. A thoughtfully downsized home can still reflect your personal style and provide comfort.

"Downsizing is for extreme minimalists."

Downsizing isn't about extremes—it's about living a more balanced life with things that serve a purpose and bring joy.

MY TOP 5 SECRETS FOR SUCCESSFUL DECLUTTERING AND DOWNSIZING

1. **Start small.** Complete one area at a time to build momentum and motivation.
2. **Sort into categories.** Use three piles—keep, donate, discard—to help you be more intentional and decisive.
3. **Acknowledge the emotional aspect.** Letting go can be painful, but remember: memories live in your heart, not in objects.
4. **Focus on clarity and freedom.** A clutter-free home lets you focus on what matters most: relationships, passions, and personal growth.

Practical Steps for Decluttering

5. **Build a team.** Surround yourself with people who support your efforts and vision.

The freedom that comes with decluttering and downsizing is available to anyone, regardless of age, income, or lifestyle. It's not just for minimalists—it's for everyone who wants to live a more intentional and fulfilling life.

Remember, downsizing isn't just about getting rid of things. It's about living a life aligned with your values and goals. It's about freedom, clarity, and simplicity.

JOURNAL PROMPTS

- ♦ The Emotional Tether Test: If you had to move abroad in 30 days with only a suitcase, what five sentimental items would you bring? What does this reveal about what truly matters to you?

Quick Exercise
The "Last Time" Experiment:

- ♦ Walk through your home and pick up five random items.
- ♦ Ask yourself: When was the last time I used this? When will I realistically use it again?
- ♦ If your answer is uncertain or in the distant future, place it in a "Release Box."
- ♦ At the end of the week, reflect on whether you missed anything in the box. If not, donate or discard them.

Quick Tips

1. **"The Stranger's Home Test:"** Imagine your home belongs to someone else, and you are visiting for the first time. What objects would stand out as unnecessary clutter? Which ones feel essential? This fresh perspective can help you make unbiased decluttering decisions.

2. **"Create a 'Clutter-Free Me' Mantra:"** Identify the #1 emotion clutter brings into your life (e.g., stress, guilt, stagnation). Now, create a mantra that flips that narrative (e.g., "I release the weight of the past to embrace the lightness of now"). Repeat it every time you struggle to let go.

3. **"Decluttering Karma:"** For every item you donate, write down one way that act of letting go could improve someone else's life (e.g., "This coat will keep someone warm this winter"). This shifts your focus from loss to contribution, making the process more meaningful.

Practical Steps for Decluttering

NOTES:

Rita Wilkins, "The Downsizing Designer"

If you have been putting off confronting your adult kids or other family members about their stuff in your basement, these tips will encourage you to practice a little tough love so you can have your house back.

Practical Steps for Decluttering

ARTICLE 4

Get Your Own House Back! Stop Being a Repository for Other People's Stuff!

If there is one thing many of us noticed during the Covid lockdown, it was the amount of clutter we had accumulated and the profound impact it had on how we felt in our own homes.

For the first time, you may have clearly felt how clutter affected your health, well-being, and relationships. You might have realized that the stress in your home—and in your life—was directly related to the sheer amount of stuff you owned. Living in close quarters for an extended time brought this reality into sharp focus.

The pandemic not only forced us to confront our own clutter but also brought attention to "other people's clutter" occupying our homes, perhaps for many years.

A WAKE-UP CALL

As you looked around, perhaps you noticed that a large portion of your basement was filled with your adult children's high school and college memorabilia—stuff they left behind for you to keep. Now, they have homes of their own, but your basement remains the repository for their things.

You may have also realized another significant part of your storage was taken up by hand-me-down furniture, clothing from well-meaning family and friends, and gifts you received but never used. At one point, you might have thought these items were "too good" to discard because you might need them "someday."

Then there's the "temporary" storage of furniture and memorabilia from the homes of deceased parents or loved ones. These sentimental items were hard to let go of while you were grieving their loss.

A CATALYST FOR CHANGE

Now, for the first time, you've realized:

- **You allowed this to happen.** Your home and storage unit became dumping grounds for other people's belongings.
- **Other people's clutter causes tension and resentment.** Without boundaries or timelines, you said "yes" to being the caretaker of others' stuff.
- **It's time to reclaim your space.** You're ready for less clutter, more peace of mind, and clear boundaries to prevent this from happening again.

You're tired of feeling guilty, resentful, and overwhelmed by the volume of stuff in your home—especially since so much of it isn't even yours. Now, you're committed to getting your own house back.

5 STEPS TO RECLAIMING SPACE IN YOUR HOME

1. Acknowledge Your Role

Recognize that you allowed this to occur. Commit to a plan to reclaim your house by setting boundaries, saying "no" when necessary, and ensuring it doesn't happen again.

2. Identify Other People's Stuff

Take inventory of items you no longer want in your home. Be clear about what needs to go and create a plan to remove it.

Practical Steps for Decluttering

3. Discern What to Keep from Loved Ones

Decide which sentimental items from deceased loved ones you truly want and will use. Donate, sell, or give away the rest to family or friends who will appreciate them.

4. Set a Plan and Timeline

Establish goals and a timeline for decluttering. Write your plan down and follow through to remove unwanted items.

5. Talk to Your Adult Children

Have an honest conversation with your adult children about their belongings. Explain that you're decluttering and may be downsizing. Give them a deadline to pick up their items and let them handle the details—whether they keep, sell, or donate. This could also be an opportunity to offer them other things you're letting go of.

TOP 3 BENEFITS OF GETTING YOUR OWN HOUSE BACK

1. Your Home Feels Lighter... and So Do You

With less stuff, your home gains a positive energy that fosters peace and clarity. You'll feel a weight lifted off your shoulders.

2. A Newfound Respect

Standing your ground and creating boundaries will not only increase your self-respect but also earn you newfound respect from others, including your children.

3. More Time, Energy, and Freedom

Decluttering your home also declutters your life, giving you more time, energy, and freedom to focus on what truly matters.

Rita Wilkins, "The Downsizing Designer"

If you're in the process of decluttering your home, you can get a free chapter of Rita's best-selling book, *Downsize Your Life, Upgrade Your Lifestyle!*

Practical Steps for Decluttering

JOURNAL PROMPTS

- ♦ How does having other people's belongings in your home affect your sense of ownership and peace?
- ♦ Are there any items in your home that belong to someone else? How can you respectfully ask them to reclaim their things?

Quick Exercise

The 3-Box Method: Label three boxes— "Keep," "Give Away," and "Return." Go through any items in your home that don't belong to you and place them in the appropriate box.

Quick Tip

Let go of the guilt. Returning or donating items that aren't yours creates space for your own life and energy.

NOTES:

_____
_____
_____
_____
_____
_____
_____
_____
_____
_____
_____
_____
_____

Rita Wilkins, "The Downsizing Designer"

If you are at a crossroads, rethinking your next steps, and if you have never heard of a reverse bucket list, I suggest you try it.

You'll gain new insights by looking back on your life, the lessons you've learned, and people who have influenced you along the way. It's the perfect tool to help you think differently and inspire a different perspective on your own life.

ARTICLE 5

How a Reverse Bucket List Can Reboot and Reignite Your Life and Career

One of the most talked-about subjects of our time, especially at this stage of our lives, is how to successfully navigate uncertain times so we can not only survive but thrive. In Bruce Feiler's book, Life Is in the Transitions, he refers to times of great upheaval and uncertainty as "Life Quakes."

He defines them as massive life changes, either voluntary or involuntary, that cause us to dig deeply and think differently so we can come out on the other side stronger and better.

THE GIFT OF TIME

The years after 60 can be a wonderful opportunity to slow down, rethink, and reconsider "what's next." They give us the "gift" of time—one that we have never experienced before. By embracing this pause, we can be more intentional as we pivot from the life we have been living to the life we've dreamed about.

This is, of course, the life we put on the back burner or on our "someday" list. It's the life filled with passion, purpose, and meaning.

Now, more than ever before, is the perfect time to reimagine, reboot, and reignite our lives and careers so that our Third Act is our best act yet—in spite of all we might be going through.

5 STATEMENTS TO CONSIDER

Have you found yourself saying one of these:

- ♦ "Life is just too short, and I'm running out of time to follow my dreams."
- ♦ "I just can't do this (job) anymore."
- ♦ "I've been asking myself if this is all there is."
- ♦ "I want and need so much more (fulfillment, joy, happiness)."
- ♦ "It's time for me—finally!"

Just like you, many midlife women are facing similar "Life Quakes," some by their own choosing and some thrust upon them.

THE LIFE QUAKES WE FACE

Demanding Career

Perhaps you have chosen to leave an extremely fast-paced, "always-on" career that, while financially rewarding, is physically and emotionally draining. You are now ready to discover a more balanced lifestyle business—one that affords you more time and freedom.

Switching Direction

You would like to explore a completely new direction in your life and career—one that will make you feel fully alive and on fire, living your passion, purpose, and the "why that makes you cry."

New Reality

You are faced with a sudden new reality: job loss, the death of a spouse, or a serious diagnosis. You want to—or have to—reengage in the workforce to supplement your income.

Practical Steps for Decluttering

Facing Fear

You are in unfamiliar territory. You're afraid. You're stuck. You know you have to do something, but you don't know how. Change is never easy, so how can you turn these challenges into opportunities?

What Is a Reverse Bucket List?

We are all familiar with the Traditional Bucket List (TBL)—that well-worn list that helps us step out of our comfort zones and pushes us to do things we've always wanted to do but never thought we would... or could.

The TBL is aspirational and great for moving us forward. However, it can leave us feeling guilty, reminding us of all the things we still haven't done. It's like having a "to-do" list hanging over our heads.

Conversely, the Reverse Bucket List (RBL) is inspirational. It helps us Reflect and focus on all we have already accomplished in life, including the big things and the important "little things"—things that make us proud, lessons we've learned, and experiences and people that have shaped who we are today and given our lives meaning.

An RBL allows us to acknowledge ourselves and to be grateful for who we are and who we have become. It boosts self-esteem, provides perspective, and serves as a great reminder when we feel discouraged.

The RBL is a motivational tool that helps you reconnect with the dreams you once had but might have forgotten. It inspires you to create new goals by identifying when you were happiest and most fulfilled so you can replicate or create new experiences like those that gave your life meaning.

The RBL can be an invaluable catalyst to see your life through a new lens, enabling you to think differently as you create a bold new vision for the life you want while carving out "what's next" in your future.

WHY DO YOU NEED A REVERSE BUCKET LIST?

Here are my top 10 ways you can use an RBL to reignite and reboot your life and career:

1. Appreciation

Reflect on your personal and professional goals and experiences, the lives you've impacted, the obstacles you've overcome, and your proudest moments. These can provide newfound appreciation, gratitude, and respect for all you've already accomplished.

2. Validation

Acknowledge the hard-earned skills that helped you move forward despite challenges. Connect what you most enjoy doing with your passion, purpose, and unique gifts.

3. Clarity

Consider these questions:

- What did you fight for?
- Which values are non-negotiable?
- What is the "why that makes you cry?"

4. Insight and Perspective

- What were you doing when you lost all track of time?
- When did you feel most fulfilled, regardless of whether you were compensated?
- What surprised you the most?

Practical Steps for Decluttering

5. Deeper Connection
- What do you want more of in your life? Why don't you have it now?
- What do you want less of? Are there things you need to let go of?
- What do you yearn for that you don't have now?

6. Vision and Blueprint
Start dreaming again without limits. Big dreams, little dreams. New dreams, old dreams. Design the life you want now.

7. Inspiration
Create goals that match your vision. Commit to a plan of action and create a realistic timeline to implement it.

8. Living Life on the Skinny Branches
Step out of your comfort zone. Do what scares you. Stop playing small. This will lead you to the life you want so you can live with no regrets.

9. Support
Surround yourself with like-minded people who will support and challenge you. They will help you brainstorm ideas, expand your dreams and goals, and hold you accountable.

10. Celebrate
Finally, celebrate the promise of your new life—the one you get to design. A life that is meaningful, fulfilling, and allows you to make a difference not just for yourself but for others.

If you want to thrive in your Third Act and live the life you really want, now is the perfect time to reboot and reignite your life and career.

Rita Wilkins, "The Downsizing Designer"

Regardless of your situation, when you rediscover your passion and purpose, you'll utilize your unique gifts, talents, and resources while living a life of freedom, fulfillment, and joy—a life where work feels like play, where you make a good income and a big impact, and where you can hardly wait to start your day!

Practical Steps for Decluttering

JOURNAL PROMPTS

- **Think about the lessons you've learned from life's "Life Quakes."** How have they shaped your view of yourself and your goals?

- **Write down three accomplishments or experiences you are most proud of.** How can you leverage those in your current or future life/career?

- **What do you yearn for but have yet to make space for?** What's one small step you could take today to bring more of that into your life?

- **When did you feel the most free in your life?** How can you create more of that freedom moving forward?

Quick Exercise

The Reverse Bucket List Reflection:

- Take 10 minutes to list at least 5 major life events or achievements that made you proud.

- For each item, jot down how it shaped you—either personally or professionally.

- Consider what made you happiest during those times. What were the circumstances around those moments of joy and fulfillment?

- From this list, identify themes or patterns that highlight what truly matters to you and might help guide your future decisions.

Quick Tip

Reframe "Unfinished" Goals: Instead of feeling burdened by unachieved aspirations, treat them as starting points for new opportunities. Your Reverse Bucket List can inspire you to reinvent old dreams and breathe new life into them.

NOTES:

CHAPTER III
Emotional and Legacy Considerations

It might hurt when our kids tell us they don't want our stuff, but it is far more important to open the door to conversations and stories that will be far more memorable and valuable than our possessions.

ARTICLE 1

"Mom, Thanks, But No Thanks!"
The Rebellion Against Family Heirlooms

There was a time when heirs eagerly anticipated inheriting their parents' and grandparents' most prized possessions—fine bone china, lead crystal, and sterling silver. These items were welcomed, proudly displayed, and even regularly used.

If there wasn't room in our homes, we stored them in attics or basements, preserving them to pass on to our kids someday.

But today, if you have adult children, you've likely realized they don't want these things—and that hurts.

SENTIMENTAL ITEMS: THE HEARTBREAK OF UNWANTED HEIRLOOMS

You've loved these items, used them, and cared for them. You looked forward to giving them to your children one day. You've held onto them for years, believing they would need and cherish these items once they had homes of their own.

Yet, for the most part, they don't want them.

Why not? What changed?

As baby boomers, now in the process of downsizing and decluttering, we face a harsh reality: our kids don't value our belongings the way we do.

A HISTORICAL PERSPECTIVE

Understanding generational values, tastes, and priorities sheds light on why younger generations resist heirlooms. These changes reflect shifting attitudes toward physical possessions, sentimentality, and practicality.

Emotional and Legacy Considerations

Bridging this gap between our sentimental attachment and their minimalist preferences requires empathy and adaptation.

GENERATIONAL DIFFERENCES

Traditionalists/Silent Generation (Born 1928–1945)

Shaped by the Great Depression and World War II, this generation valued frugality, practicality, and resourcefulness. Their few possessions were cherished for their utility and longevity.

Baby Boomers (Born 1946–1964)

Boomers grew up during post-war prosperity, embracing consumerism. To them, material goods signified success, status, and security. However, this focus on accumulating possessions often came at the cost of work-life balance.

Generation X (Born 1965–1980)

Gen Xers were influenced by early technology and the rise of social media. While they appreciate material goods, they value experiences and minimalism, seeking a balance between hard work and living fully.

Millennials (Born 1981–1996)

Having grown up in the Digital Age, Millennials prioritize experiences, sustainability, and minimalist living. They view "stuff" as clutter, favoring meaningful work and balance over material possessions.

Generation Z (Born 1997–2012)

Born into the Digital Age, Gen Z values individuality, sustainability, and authenticity. They prefer borrowing, renting, or repurposing items rather than accumulating possessions.

Rita Wilkins, "The Downsizing Designer"

Times Have Changed

What we value as sentimental, our kids often see as clutter. Let's examine some key differences between baby boomers and younger generations.

Physical Possessions

Younger generations prioritize a minimalist aesthetic. To them, excess "stuff" feels overwhelming.

Emotional Attachment

Unlike us, they feel little emotional attachment to physical possessions, viewing them as replaceable.

Smaller Homes and Living Spaces

Younger generations prefer smaller homes, making it impractical to inherit large furniture or collections.

Experiences Over Stuff

They value spending money on experiences, prioritizing memories over material goods.

Sustainability

Younger generations emphasize sustainability, choosing to buy less and reduce waste.

BRIDGING THE GAP

Despite these differences, there's common ground. Baby boomers and younger generations share an appreciation for simplicity, intentional living, and meaningful experiences.

Emotional and Legacy Considerations

Steps to Bridge the Gap
1. **Take an Inventory**

   Assess what you need, use, and want. Consider what ts into your current lifestyle and future plans.

2. **Open Conversations**

   Invite your kids to share what they do and don't want. Share stories about family heirlooms to help them appreciate their value.

3. **Invite Family and Friends**

   Offer unwanted items to family and friends before donating or disposing of them.

4. **Donate or Dispose**

   Donate items to charities or responsibly dispose of what remains.

FINDING COMMON GROUND

Preserving our family heritage isn't just about passing down physical items. It's about taking time to share stories and our values too.

By finding common ground between our sentimental side and their desire to redefine how family treasures are passed down, we can ensure that our family legacy will live on long after we're gone.

Let's embrace this challenge, consider it a teaching moment, an opportunity to listen, learn, and grow closer to our kids by having meaningful conversations where both sides are heard… knowing that together, we are keeping the spirit and essence of our family alive for many generations to come.

JOURNAL PROMPTS

Reflect on the values, traditions, and lessons you'd like to pass on to future generations. How can you share these legacies in ways beyond physical possessions?

Quick Exercise

Heirloom Inventory Check

Select three items you consider heirlooms or sentimental keepsakes. For each item, ask:

- ♦ *Do I use this regularly?*
- ♦ *Does it bring me joy?*
- ♦ *Will it be meaningful to someone else?*

Decide whether to keep, gift, donate, or repurpose each item.

Quick Tips

- ♦ **Start Small**

    Begin with one category of items (e.g., china, photo albums, or furniture). Breaking it into smaller steps prevents overwhelm.

- ♦ **Tell the Story**

    Share the history or significance of heirlooms with your family. The story might make them more meaningful to someone else—or help you let go.

- ♦ **Find New Homes**

    Offer items to friends, extended family, or donation centers that can honor their value. Knowing they're appreciated can ease the separation process.

Emotional and Legacy Considerations

NOTES:

Rita Wilkins, "The Downsizing Designer"

Don't be upset if your kids reject your family heirlooms. Give them a new life at a secondhand store.

Emotional and Legacy Considerations

ARTICLE 2

It's Just Grandma's Old Stuff... Until It's Vintage. Then It's Chic!

Just two weeks prior, I produced a viral YouTube video: *"Mom, Thanks but No Thanks: The Rebellion Against Family Heirlooms."* Watched by tens of thousands of millennials, Gen Xers, and Baby Boomers alike, it sparked a meaningful dialogue about what to do with inherited items that younger generations simply don't want.

Here's the twist: While younger generations may turn their noses up at some family heirlooms, they're flocking to thrift shops and vintage stores in search of treasures. The same millennials and Gen Zers who say "No thanks" to mom's china are now saying "Yes, please" to unique, high-quality vintage furniture and clothing.

This cultural shift is redefining what it means to cherish the past. Let's explore why new-age thrift shopping is booming and how it's changing the narrative around family heirlooms.

WHY DON'T THEY WANT OUR STUFF?

As members of older generations, we often feel challenged—physically and emotionally—about what to do with the many things we've accumulated over the past decades, along with items inherited from our parents and grandparents.

In the past, younger generations were eager to receive treasured family heirlooms. Today, however, they're more likely to say, "Thanks, but no thanks," for reasons like:

- **Smaller living spaces:** Many younger people live in smaller homes and don't have room for heirlooms.
- **Minimalist lifestyles:** They prefer keeping only what they love, need, and use.
- **Different tastes:** Today's aesthetics often clash with our "big brown furniture."

THE GOOD NEWS

If your kids don't want your stuff, don't worry—someone else does! Thanks to Gen Z, secondhand shopping has gone mainstream. This trend reflects a shift toward sustainable, high-quality, and affordable alternatives.

In 2023, a Pew Research study revealed:

- **42% of Gen Z and 39% of millennials** shopped in secondhand stores.
- **59%** said they planned to shop secondhand more often.

This shift means your cherished items can find new homes where they'll be loved and appreciated, keeping the history alive and reducing landfill waste. It's a win-win for everyone.

Who's Buying Our Old Stuff?

- **Young professionals:** Furnishing first apartments with secondhand finds.
- **Young families:** Tight budgets lead them to secondhand shops for affordable furniture and clothing.
- **Baby boomers:** Many of my friends frequent vintage stores for unique clothing and decor.

Emotional and Legacy Considerations

As an interior designer, I've found incredible bargains on high-end furniture for client projects. Even I became a "believer" in resale shopping when I discovered my favorite winter coat at a resale store for a fraction of its retail price. It's no longer just "used"—it's *repurposed*.

GETTING STARTED WITH SECONDHAND SHOPPING

Key Terms to Know

- **Secondhand stores:** Profit-based, buying and selling good used items.
- **Consignment shops:** Commission-based, taking a percentage for selling items.
- **Thrift stores:** Donation-based, proceeds go to charity.

Online Options

- Facebook Marketplace
- The RealReal (for vintage designer brands)
- ThredUp, Poshmark, and Kaiyo

Circular Economy

Keeping items in circulation reduces land fill waste and promotes sustainability.

Upcycling

Repurposing items (e.g., sanding and painting furniture) minimizes waste and reduces the carbon footprint.

HOW TO SELL OR DONATE YOUR STUFF

Selling or Consigning

1. **Inventory and photos:** Create a list with measurements and clear photos.
2. **Research:** Visit local resale shops to gauge interest and understand policies.
3. **Pricing:** Be realistic; items may take time to sell or fetch less than you expect.

Donating

1. **Find a cause:** Research charities that align with your values (e.g., Habitat for Humanity, Ministry of Caring).
2. **Drop-off or pick-up:** Some organizations offer home pickups for large items.
3. **Tax receipt:** Ensure you receive documentation for tax purposes.

ONE FINAL THOUGHT

Even though your kids don't want your stuff, isn't it comforting to know that somewhere, someone is cherishing your grandma's old table as their new treasure? Together, we're redefining what it means to give the past a future.

Emotional and Legacy Considerations

JOURNAL PROMPTS

- ◆ Reflect on an item you've held onto for sentimental reasons. How does it make you feel? Could it bring joy to someone else?
- ◆ What does the term "vintage" mean to you? How does it differ from "old" in your mind?
- ◆ Write about a time you found joy in repurposing or upcycling something. What made it special??

Quick Exercise

- ◆ **Heirloom Inventory Check:** Take 15 minutes to identify five items in your home that you no longer use or need. Decide whether to sell, donate, or repurpose them. Create a plan for their next chapter.

Quick Tips

- ◆ **Be patient:** Thrift shopping requires time and persistence, but the rewards are worth it.
- ◆ **Get creative:** Explore upcycling projects to breathe new life into old items.

NOTES:

_____
_____
_____
_____
_____
_____
_____
_____

Rita Wilkins, "The Downsizing Designer"

Believe it or not, it is possible to find common ground in this age-old dispute. Here's how!

Emotional and Legacy Considerations

ARTICLE 3

What Do You Do When You Want to Downsize— But Your Spouse Doesn't?

As an interior designer for over 35 years, I've had the privilege of helping baby boomers design their first, second, and even third homes, as well as their beach houses, mountain retreats, and country cottages. I've guided them through upsizing to larger homes (because that's what baby boomers did!) and now, at this stage of life, many are deciding whether to age in place, right-size, or downsize.

The irony is, after years of helping clients upsize and acquire more, I now assist them in downsizing, decluttering, and parting with the items they've accumulated or inherited.

Many baby boomers still cling to the belief that "more is better." They struggle with letting go of their big houses, cherished memories made around their kitchen tables, and beautiful collections amassed over the years. On the other hand, some boomers are excited to embrace a simpler life in a smaller, more manageable home that offers less stress and more freedom.

But what happens when one spouse is ready to downsize and the other isn't?

DOWNSIZING IS A MATTER OF CHOICE

At first glance, this might seem like an impossible situation, where one partner's wishes must outweigh the other's. But it doesn't have to be that way!

Throughout my career, I've often found myself mediating these sometimes-heated discussions, embracing the role of neutral middleman to help both partners find common ground. With the right approach, couples can redefine what "having it all" means to them and determine compromises that work for both.

By asking key questions and fostering open communication, it's possible to move toward a win-win solution. If you're struggling with a downsizing dilemma, these seven tips can help:

1. Hear Others' Stories

It's rarely productive to keep the discussion between yourselves. Reach out to family, friends, or colleagues who have successfully downsized, right-sized, or chosen to age in place. Ask them:

- What were their experiences, both good and bad?
- How did they make their decision?
- What obstacles or fears did they face, and how did they overcome them?
- Are they happy with their choice?
- What advice would they give to others?

Learning from others' experiences can o er valuable perspectives and reduce uncertainty.

2. Talk It Out

Have an honest conversation where both partners share their thoughts, feelings, and concerns. Each should:

- List reasons for wanting to stay (e.g., memories, neighborhood) or move (e.g., more freedom, less stress).
- Address fears of moving (e.g., fear of change) or staying (e.g., increasing maintenance costs).
- Highlight areas where they're willing to compromise and where they're not.

Emotional and Legacy Considerations

Discussing these openly can uncover underlying motivations and help identify common ground.

3. Know What You Want

Before making any decisions, create a shared vision for your future lifestyle. Consider:

- What would life look like if you downsized? What if you stayed?
- Are there similarities between your visions?
- Can you test potential solutions, such as decluttering first or renting a smaller place temporarily?

4. Do Your Due Diligence

Analyze the pros and cons of each option, including the financial implications:

- Staying: Consider costs like roof replacement, ongoing maintenance, and renovations for aging in place.
- Moving: Factor in expenses like buying, renting, and moving costs.

Having a clear picture of the financial impact can help guide your decision.

5. Prototype and Try Different Lifestyles

Before making a permanent move, experiment with different living arrangements. Take extended vacations to areas you're curious about, such as city living, community living, or being closer to family. These trials can provide valuable insights and reduce the fear of the unknown.

6. Rent for a Period of Time

Consider renting a smaller home for a few months. This limited-time commitment allows you to test the waters without making an irreversible decision.

7. Phase Your Decision by Decluttering First

Start by editing and decluttering your current home. Sell, donate, or consign items that no longer serve a purpose. By experiencing life with less, you may find greater clarity about your next steps.

Communication Is Key

The best way to navigate a downsizing disagreement is to keep an open mind and communicate honestly. Share your concerns as well as your hopes and dreams. Ultimately, the goal is to design a new life that you both love together.

Emotional and Legacy Considerations

JOURNAL PROMPTS
- What does your ideal future home look like? How does it make you feel?
- What are three things you value most about your current home? What are three things you could do without?
- What fears do you have about downsizing or staying? How can you address them?

Quick Exercise
Heirloom Inventory Check
- Take 10 minutes to walk through your home with your spouse.
- Each of you chooses three items you could let go of and share why. (This small step can open up a productive dialogue about decluttering.)

Quick Tips
- Declutter one room or category at a time.
- Focus on shared goals, like reducing stress or saving money.
- Celebrate small victories together, such as donating a box of items or organizing a closet.

NOTES:
_____
_____
_____
_____
_____

*Memories are made of the moments we share.
They are the gifts we give that will last for generations.*

Emotional and Legacy Considerations

ARTICLE 4

Leave a Lasting Legacy: It's What We Do, Not What We Have

A lasting legacy isn't about the material possessions we accumulate—it's about the impact we make through our actions and the memories we create. The greatest legacy we can leave our children is happy memories rooted in shared experiences, love, and laughter.

REFLECTION: WHAT TRULY MATTERS?

When you look back on your life, who or what has shaped you the most? Was it a cherished heirloom, or was it the shared experiences that left an indelible mark on your soul?

For me, it was almost always the latter. One of my most cherished memories is sitting at the kitchen table with my Polish grandmother, learning how to pinch pierogies. Beyond the technique, I absorbed her lessons of perseverance, faith, and grit. She gave me more than just her recipe—she shared her spirit.

WHY INTANGIBLE HEIRLOOMS MATTER

Bridging Generations

An intangible legacy—memories, traditions, and life lessons—bridges the generational gap. It creates connections that transcend physical possessions.

Rethinking Family Heirlooms

Rather than focusing solely on material objects, consider the value of passing down family stories, traditions, and experiences that create lasting bonds.

Enriching Lives

Shared moments foster deeper relationships and lay a foundation for future generations to honor family values and traditions.

30 OPPORTUNITIES TO CONNECT GENERATIONS

From baking together to bedtime stories, here are ways to create meaningful moments that will be remembered long after possessions fade.

1. Cooking and Baking Together

Food is love. It's a powerful way to connect generations, teach new skills, and create lasting memories—like baking Christmas cookies, making pierogi, or molding butter lambs for Easter.

2. Holiday Gatherings

Celebrating holidays together creates opportunities to share food, fun, memories, and traditions (e.g., Christmas, Easter, Thanksgiving, Hanukkah).

3. Family Celebrations

Sharing significant events together, both happy and sad, strengthens family bonds, connecting us on a deeper level (e.g., weddings, funerals, graduations).

4. Family Dinners

There's no place like the kitchen table to share, learn, ask advice, and exchange ideas. This teaches us the importance of family.

Emotional and Legacy Considerations

5. Multigenerational Travel

Exploring new places, people, and cultures with parents, grandparents, and kids opens doors to conversations while sharing food, fun, and creating new memories.

6. Family Vacations

Taking time to be together, having fun, relaxing, and learning generates many opportunities to have great conversations and create new memories together (e.g., beach, mountain vacations).

7. Sports

Participating in sports together provides opportunities to learn new skills, spend time together, and have fun (e.g., golf, pickleball, tennis, swimming, walking, running).

8. Sporting Events

Watching sports together provides opportunities to share a love of a particular sport, generating conversation and bonding (e.g., football, baseball, soccer, lacrosse).

9. Hobbies

Doing hobbies together provides opportunities to learn new skills, develop common interests, and have fun creating something together (e.g., sewing, crafting, woodworking).

10. Arts and Entertainment

Various entertainment mediums provide opportunities to experience something new together, enjoy time together, and connect on a deeper level (e.g., theater, museums).

11. Gardening

Working in the yard provides an opportunity to share a love of nature, develop new skills, and learn to care for and nurture what we grow together (e.g., flower gardens, vegetable gardens).

12. Household Chores

Sharing responsibilities for a household, contributing to your family, whether young or old creates bonds (e.g., doing the dishes, setting the table).

13. Church and Spiritual Activities

Connect with your loved ones on a spiritual level, sharing your faith and beliefs, traditions, and customs (e.g., church on Sundays, celebrating spiritual holidays).

14. Volunteering

Sharing your time and your gifts with others helps foster compassion and commitment to helping those in need (e.g., Meals on Wheels, serving food at a homeless shelter).

15. Classes

Incorporating learning into our lives teaches the value of sharing knowledge, wisdom, and exchanging ideas so young and old can learn from each other (e.g., language, technology, cooking).

16. Music

Music is a universal language that connects young and old (e.g., everyone singing around the piano).

Emotional and Legacy Considerations

17. Granny and Grandpa Camp

Overnights at your home to spend time together, tell stories, learn about your family history and traditions, and receive advice and mentorship.

18. Bedtime Stories

This evening ritual and commitment is an opportunity to spend quality time together, connect on a much deeper level, and learn from books or family stories.

19. Writing and Journaling

Taking time to record family memories, stories, and exchange ideas creates respect for our past and learning about our roots.

20. Movie Night

Teaches the importance of shared time and experiences, laughing, crying, and having fun together.

21. Board Games and Card Games

Having fun, friendly competition teaches the value of family time together across all generations.

22. Handyman Projects/Repairs

Handywork teaches valuable life skills that we can incorporate into our own lives. It also offers quality time together to have important conversations and share family values.

23. Competitions

Competing is a healthy way to have fun together, create new memories through meaningful experiences, and teach discipline, sacrifice, and perseverance (e.g., 5k walks, marathons).

24. Family Photos

Looking at family photos together inspires conversations, sharing stories that help preserve cherished memories. It also provides an opportunity to learn about our family history and connect to our roots.

25. Finances and Investing

Discussing finances and investing is an opportunity to advise, mentor, and plan for the future. It also teaches discipline, sacrifice, and commitment to goals.

26. Technology

This is an opportunity for the younger generation to share their knowledge and skills with the older generation, teaching them that we all learn from each other.

27. FaceTime

This is an opportunity to stay in touch regardless of the distance, sharing about our lives together.

28. Treasure Hunts in Grandma's Attic

Looking through the attic creates an opportunity to explore family heirlooms, listen to family stories, and ask questions about your roots. This opens our eyes to family treasures, connecting us on a much deeper level.

29. Crafting

Sharing an activity you love, teaching new skills, and creating something together is a unique bonding experience.

Emotional and Legacy Considerations

30. Emails and Texts

This provides an opportunity to stay connected, regardless of the distance, sharing what's happening in your lives. The result is a continuous bond.

FINAL REFLECTION: STUFF DOES NOT REMAIN

When we die, our possessions will be left behind and most won't be cherished. What we will be remembered for will be:

- ♦ The love we shared.
- ♦ The laughter we brought.
- ♦ The lives we've touched.
- ♦ The memories we've made.

Take time to reflect on the impact you want to leave behind. Prioritize actions that can change lives by the way you live each day. The experiences you create with your kids and grandkids today will not only impact their present fun and enjoyment, but they will also impact the future memories they have and the stories they will tell for many years to come.

FINAL THOUGHTS: LOVE, LAUGHTER, AND LEGACY

At the end of our lives, it won't be the possessions we leave behind that matter most—it will be the love, laughter, and memories we've shared. By focusing on intangible heirlooms, we can ensure that our legacy lives on in the hearts and minds of those we cherish. Start small. Each shared moment, story, or tradition is a step toward leaving a meaningful, lasting legacy.

JOURNAL PROMPTS

Reflect on a memory with a loved one that shaped who you are today. How can you create similar experiences for your children or grandchildren?

Quick Exercise

- Take 10 minutes to write down three traditions or shared activities you loved as a child.
- Next, brainstorm how you can recreate or adapt these for your family today.

Quick Tips

- **Focus on Shared Experiences:** Prioritize spending time together over giving material gifts.
- **Preserve Stories:** Record family stories in a journal or digital format to share with future generations.
- **Be Present:** The most valuable gift you can give your loved ones is your time and attention.

NOTES:

_____
_____
_____
_____
_____
_____
_____

Emotional and Legacy Considerations

Faced with a sudden, life-altering change, how will you respond? Will you choose to thrive or merely survive?

ARTICLE 5

Dare to Dream Again After Being Hit by a Life Quake

At some point in your life, you will go through "something." That "something" could be the sudden death of a loved one, a painful divorce, an unexpected financial crisis, or another dreaded life event.

LIFE QUAKES

These "life quakes" are transformative experiences that alter our reality overnight. Our world is suddenly turned upside down. The foundation and security we once knew vanish, leaving us to ask, "Why me, God?"

Life quakes leave you with more questions than answers:

- ♦ *Who am I now?*
- ♦ *How will I ever survive this crisis, let alone thrive?*

You may feel afraid, confused, uncertain, and unprepared for what comes next.

Mourning the loss of your previous life and saying goodbye to the way things were takes time. But as you come face-to-face with your new reality and it begins to settle in, you realize you must do something.

But *what*? And *how*?

NAVIGATING LIFE TRANSITIONS

Life transitions are never easy. They are rarely linear and often require time and thoughtful introspection.

Emotional and Legacy Considerations

Do you just "carry on" and adapt to your new life as a widow or divorcee? Do you look for another job similar to your previous one simply because it's a safe choice? Or...

Do you see this "life quake" as a fork in the road—an opportunity to shake up your life, change directions, and create something new, exciting, and fulfilling? Something you dreamed of but never thought possible?

REDISCOVER YOUR PURPOSE AND LEARN TO DREAM BIG

These life-changing moments challenge you to rethink, reimagine, and redefine who you are and what you want to become.

Do you:

- ♦ Continue to hold on to the status quo because it's the most comfortable choice? Or...
- ♦ Choose to look forward, embrace this time of change, and intentionally redesign your life into something you've always dreamed of?

The choice is yours.

If you choose to reinvent yourself after a "life quake," allow yourself to dream big.

LIVES CHANGE. DREAMS CHANGE.

What are your new dreams?

Step 1: Discern What Matters Most to You Right Now ... And *Why*

Start by asking yourself what matters most to you now and why. Your life has changed, and likely, so have your interests and priorities. Pause and gain perspective on what you value most today. This will be the foundation for your future decisions.

Step 2: Create a Vision for What You Want Your Life to Look Like

Prioritize yourself. It's not selfish—it's self-care.

Ask yourself:

- ♦ What makes you happy?
- ♦ What gives your life meaning?
- ♦ What lights you up?

With those answers in mind, dream. Dream some more. And dream BIG. Let nothing constrain your dreams.

Step 3: Let Go of What Holds You Back

Pursuing your new dreams requires determination and the courage to shed fears and limiting beliefs. Once you shift your mindset, you begin to see life through a lens of possibilities. Your vision for a new life becomes clearer, and you start believing your dreams are achievable.

It takes courage to endure life quakes, to begin again, and to embrace change. But once you dare to dream and give yourself permission to pursue those dreams, there's no stopping you!

Emotional and Legacy Considerations

JOURNAL PROMPTS
- Have you experienced a life quake?
- Have you embraced it as an opportunity to redesign your life?
- What dreams have I put on hold, and why?
- What is one small step I can take today to move toward my new vision?
- What limiting beliefs do I need to release to create space for new possibilities?

Quick Exercise
- Take 10 minutes to write a vision statement for your life one year from now. Be as specific as possible. Include how you want to feel, where you want to be, and what you'll be doing.

Quick Tips
- Break your dreams into manageable steps to avoid feeling overwhelmed.
- Surround yourself with people who uplift and encourage your growth.
- Acknowledge and celebrate every step forward, no matter how small.

NOTES:
_____
_____
_____
_____
_____

CHAPTER IV

Lifestyle Design (Minimalist's Mindset)

How is decision fatigue impacting your daily life?

Use these proven strategies to streamline your choices, reduce overwhelm, and improve your ability to make quicker, more confident decisions.

Lifestyle Design (Minimalist's Mindset)

ARTICLE 1

5 Top Secrets to Beat Decision Fatigue with Fewer Choices

Do you feel overwhelmed by the countless decisions you face every day? From the moment you crawl out of bed to the time you rest your head on the pillow at night, *Psychology Today* estimates that we make more than **2,000 decisions every working hour**—one every two seconds! And that's just an average day.

Now, imagine trying to **downsize**, **declutter**, or **redesign your kitchen**. It's no wonder decision fatigue creeps in.

In our fast-paced world, where endless streams of information and too many choices bombard us daily, **decision fatigue** is a real challenge. This phenomenon doesn't just sap your energy; it can also affect your emotional and mental well-being.

SIGNS OF DECISION FATIGUE

When faced with too many choices, decision fatigue manifests in various ways:

- Feeling overwhelmed, anxious, or hopeless
- Difficulty focusing
- Mental and physical exhaustion
- Brain fog
- Avoidance and procrastination
- Impulsive or rash decisions
- Irritability, especially with your own indecisiveness

WHAT TRIGGERS DECISION FATIGUE?

1. **Information Overload**

   Endless information from the internet, social media, TV, and ads can overwhelm even the most decisive individuals.

2. **Too Many Choices**

   Options are great, but when there are too many, they lead to confusion and indecision.

3. **Perfectionism**

   Expecting perfection often results in overthinking, overanalyzing, and overcomplicating decisions. This creates anxiety, frustration, and fear of making the wrong choice.

THE 5 SECRETS TO BEAT DECISION FATIGUE

Secret #1: Set Clear Goals

Clear goals help you prioritize decisions and narrow down your options. By knowing what you want to accomplish, you can focus on what truly matters.

EXAMPLE: THE ABCS OF DOWNSIZING

When helping clients downsize, I use this simple method:

A Items: Must-haves that will definitely go to your new, smaller home.

B Items: Nice-to-haves that you'd take if they fit and work well in the new space.

C Items: Things you don't need, want, or use—these can be donated, recycled, or discarded.

Lifestyle Design (Minimalist's Mindset)

Secret #2: Create Daily Routines and Habits

Automating routine decisions through daily habits conserves mental energy and reduces the number of choices you make.

EXAMPLE: CAPSULE WARDROBE

A small, versatile wardrobe simplifies your daily clothing decisions. Mixing and matching fewer items reduces stress and decision fatigue.

Secret #3: Filter Your Options

Eliminate unrealistic or non-viable options to simplify your decision-making process.

EXAMPLE: BUDGET FILTER

Set a clear budget for significant decisions, such as vacations, home renovations, or big purchases. This instantly narrows down options that don't fit your financial limits.

Secret #4: Streamline Choices—The Magic of 3

Narrowing your options to three viable choices makes it easier to compare and decide.

EXAMPLE: DESIGN OPTIONS

For my design clients, I present **three solid options** tailored to their needs:

> **Option 1:** Keeps the current structure.

> **Option 2:** Remove one wall to create an open-plan design.

> **Option 3:** Remove two walls for a fully open space. Each option comes with a distinct budget and outcome, empowering clients to decide what works best for their lifestyle.

Secret #5: Timing Is Everything

Research shows you're most alert and capable of making decisions **1 to 3 hours after waking up.** Save critical decisions for this time to maximize focus and minimize procrastination.

Decision fatigue doesn't have to control your life. By applying these five simple strategies, you can regain **clarity reduce**, **stress**, and **make better choices**. Whether you're decluttering your home or planning your next move, fewer choices can lead to a more fulfilling, intentional life.

Lifestyle Design (Minimalist's Mindset)

JOURNAL PROMPTS

- What are my top three goals for the next month, and how can I align my decisions with these goals?
- What choices in my daily life feel most overwhelming, and why do they stress me out?
- What does my ideal, simplified day look like? What decisions would be easier in this version of my life?

Quick Exercise

- **Spend 10 Minutes Listing**: Write down all the small and big decisions currently on your mind.
- **Categorize Each Decision:**
- Let Go Of: Decisions that are unimportant or can be left for later.
- Automate: Recurring choices that can be streamlined (e.g., meal prepping).
- Prioritize: Important decisions that align with your goals or values.
- Action Step: Commit to letting go of one decision, automating another, and taking action on one priority today.

Quick Tips

- **Limit Daily Decisions:**

    Reduce the number of decisions by planning ahead. For example, decide your meals, outfit, or workout schedule the night before.

- **Apply the 2-Minute Rule:**

    If a decision takes less than two minutes to make (e.g., responding to an email or picking a dinner recipe), decide and move on instead of overthinking.

- **Declutter Your Decision Space:**
  Organize your physical and digital environments to eliminate unnecessary choices. A tidy workspace or a streamlined inbox helps reduce mental clutter.

NOTES:

Lifestyle Design (Minimalist's Mindset)

As you grow and change, so do your life and lifestyle.

Let your home reflect who you are now and what matters most to you.

ARTICLE 2

Make Yourself at Home... in Your Own Home

Do you remember the pandemic? 2020 challenged us like never before. The Year of Covid forced us to slow down, reevaluate, and see our lives through a close-up lens. It illuminated what was working in our lives—and unmasked what wasn't, especially in our homes.

As the pandemic swept across the globe, it brought drastic changes to how we lived, worked, and connected. While life as we knew it came to a standstill, many of us were forced to rethink and redesign how we used our spaces, how we communicated, and how we lived together.

REDISCOVERING THE MEANING OF HOME

Before 2020, life may have felt like it was on autopilot. We were busy—too busy to enjoy life's little moments with loved ones. When Covid struck, we had no choice but to pause, adapt, and figure out new ways to live, work, learn, and play—all while sheltering in place.

What Was Different?

For many of us, the year brought unexpected changes:

- **We cooked meals together.**
- **We sat down for family dinners and meaningful conversations.**
- **We learned to adapt in ways we never thought possible.**

Yet, the challenges were undeniable. We:

- Transformed kitchen tables into home offices.
- Juggled homeschooling with remote work.
- Navigated endless hours of virtual communication on Zoom.

Lifestyle Design (Minimalist's Mindset)

And through it all, we learned to adapt, to grow, and to change.

Lessons from a Year at Home

As your home became the center of your life, you likely began to see it—and yourself—differently.

You may have:

- Discovered new ways to balance work, relationships, and personal time amidst the chaos.
- Developed a greater awareness of the little things you once overlooked.
- Realized how to "make do" with less and appreciate simplicity.
- Found newfound freedom and flexibility in your work-from-home routine.

You reinvented your lifestyle without even realizing it.

REIMAGINING HOME DESIGN POST-COVID

Our houses truly became our homes again. The pandemic prompted many of us to rethink what matters most and how our living spaces Reflect those priorities. Designers are now embracing this shift, creating homes that better serve our changing lifestyles.

EMERGING TRENDS FOR THE HOME OF THE FUTURE

1. **Multifunctional Spaces**

    Sliding walls, barn doors, and movable partitions allow spaces to transform seamlessly for work, learning, and relaxation.

2. **Dedicated Home Offices**

    Stylish, ergonomic home offices simulate the productivity of being at work while keeping you comfortable.

3. **Outdoor Sanctuaries**

   Patios and decks are now must-haves, offering a vital connection to nature and a mental health boost.

4. **Zoom-Ready Rooms**

   Lighting, staging, and backdrops are now as critical as the tech setup for video calls.

5. **Spa-Like Bathrooms**

   These hideaways provide the ultimate retreat for relaxation and recharging.

Your Turn: Create a Home That Nurtures You

As you reflect on how life and home have changed, ask yourself: How can your living space better Reflect your needs, values, and aspirations?

A New Chapter for Your Home

2020 taught us to adapt, grow, and find new ways to thrive. As you move forward, let these lessons guide you. Your home is not just a space—it's a Reflection of who you are and what you value.

As you change as your life changes, how will you make yourself at home in your own home?

Lifestyle Design (Minimalist's Mindset)

JOURNAL PROMPTS

- What three words describe how you want your home to feel?
- Which spaces in your home bring you joy, and which feel like cluttered chaos?
- If your home could speak, what would it say about your priorities?
- What small changes can you make today to align your home with your dream lifestyle?

Quick Exercise

- Take 15 minutes to visualize and write down your ideal day at home. Start with how you wake up and move through your day. Be specific—describe the sights, smells, and sounds of your perfect space.
- Use this vision to guide simple but impactful changes in your living environment.

Quick Tips

- **Claim Your Space**: Dedicate areas for specific purposes—working, relaxing, or connecting with family. This creates balance and reduces overwhelm.
- **Reimagine Your Surroundings**: Rearrange furniture, add plants, or use lighting to breathe new life into your rooms.
- **Purge Without Fear**: Declutter regularly. Let go of items that no longer serve you and make room for what truly brings you joy.

NOTES:

_____

_____

_____

Rita Wilkins, "The Downsizing Designer"

Downsizing isn't downgrading.

In fact, when you live with less, you'll be surprised at how little you actually need to be truly happy.

Lifestyle Design (Minimalist's Mindset)

ARTICLE 3

Living Small but Having It All

Downsizing is on the minds of many Baby Boomers right now. With that comes the concern that downsizing your home might also mean downgrading your life and lifestyle. After all, you've grown accustomed to more space, more rooms, and more closets.

HOW COULD YOU POSSIBLY LIVE WITHOUT THEM?

The reality is that most Americans use only a small percentage of the rooms in their homes. That means much of your space is either unused or not well-utilized, costing you time, money, energy—and valuable resources that could be better spent traveling, spending time with loved ones, or pursuing a new passion or business venture.

When you start to analyze just how many rooms you actively use… When you pay attention to how many areas are used to store things you no longer need or want… When you get tired of wasting time, money, and energy cleaning, organizing, and maintaining unused or poorly used portions of your home…

… downsizing not only starts to make sense, it becomes a desirable opportunity to live in a more compact space where every inch serves a purpose. By consolidating and minimizing your possessions to only what you truly want, need, use, and love, you create a home that works for you.

The funny thing is, once you downsize, you might be surprised at just how much space you truly need to live well and comfortably.

HOW TO MAKE YOUR SMALL HOME LOOK AND FEEL BIGGER

Who said small spaces have to feel small?

As an interior designer for over 35 years, I've frequently been tasked with maximizing space for my clients—not just in functionality but also in appearance. Here are my top five design tricks to make your small home look and feel bigger:

1. Max Out Every Inch of Space

- Incorporate built-ins, wall-to-wall and floor-to-ceiling, for seamless storage and display.
- Install cabinets that extend to the ceiling in kitchens, bathrooms, laundry rooms, and mudrooms.
- Transform outdoor areas into usable "rooms" like patios, decks, or balconies.

2. A Place for Everything

Declutter first, keeping only what you truly need, use, or love. Then create designated spaces for everything:

- A cabinet or drawer for keys, wallets, and glasses.
- A system for organizing bills, mail, and magazines.
- A tray for remotes near the TV and audio equipment.

3. Multi-Tasking Furniture

Choose furniture that serves multiple purposes:

- Ottomans that double as storage, coffee tables, or seating.
- Expandable tables or Murphy beds with integrated storage.

Lifestyle Design (Minimalist's Mindset)

4. Mirrors, Glass, and Lighting Are Your Best Friends

Use mirrors to Reflect light and visually expand spaces.

Opt for glass walls or partitions to create flexible privacy without closing off spaces.

Maximize natural light and incorporate layers of ambient lighting to make spaces feel larger and brighter.

5. Choose Small Scale for Big Impact

Avoid oversized furniture in small spaces. Select smaller-scale pieces to prevent overcrowding, but don't shy away from one larger statement piece to serve as a focal point.

LIVING SMALL BUT HAVING IT ALL

Downsizing is not about compromising—it's about designing a new lifestyle.

Once you downsize and embrace living with less, you'll realize you haven't given up anything. In fact, you've created more room for what truly matters:

1. Less space to clutter, making your home easier to maintain.
2. Less temptation to accumulate unnecessary items.
3. More time for relationships and creating meaningful memories.
4. More freedom to travel, enjoy family, and explore new experiences.
5. More energy for self-care, wellness, and personal growth.

As Baby Boomers, we've learned that bigger isn't always better and that more stuff doesn't equate to happiness. We've reached a point where we realize we don't need so many toilets... or shoes... or things.

Downsizing doesn't mean downgrading—it's an opportunity to live small but have it all!

Rita Wilkins, "The Downsizing Designer"

JOURNAL PROMPTS

- What are three things you could let go of today that no longer serve you?
- Describe your ideal living space. How does it Reflect your current values?
- How could downsizing your possessions positively impact your relationships or personal goals?

Quick Exercise

- Walk into one room and identify three items you haven't used in over a year. Place them in a donation box or decide on their next steps.

Quick Tips

- Before purchasing anything new, ask yourself: "Do I have space for this? Do I truly need it?"
- Keep a donation box in your home for easy decluttering as you go about your day.
- Use visual aids like Pinterest or design boards to inspire how you can transform a smaller space into a personal haven.

NOTES:

Lifestyle Design (Minimalist's Mindset)

Is house sharing in your future? Changing times call for rethinking housing options as we age.

ARTICLE 4

A Comprehensive Guide to House Sharing: Making Your Home Roommate-Ready

House sharing can bring fun and adventure to your life, but it can also be a challenge if you're unprepared. To ensure comfort for everyone, it's essential to make your home roommate-ready. This guide will help you transform your living space into a welcoming environment for shared living.

WHEN IS HOUSE SHARING A GOOD IDEA?

Recently, a friend asked if I'd be interested in house sharing and redesigning parts of her large home to prepare it for roommates. Like many single women in their 50s, 60s, and 70s, she wanted to repurpose her biggest asset to generate income and create a vibrant, supportive community as she ages.

WHY TRY HOUSE SHARING

House sharing isn't for everyone, but it's an increasingly popular option for older women seeking financial relief, community, and companionship.

Many women worry about running out of money in retirement. House sharing offers a more affordable alternative to senior living facilities and helps alleviate financial stress by splitting housing and living costs.

Isolation and loneliness are known to shorten lifespans. House sharing fosters social connections and support systems, helping women age with companionship instead of solitude.

Lifestyle Design (Minimalist's Mindset)

While house sharing isn't caregiving, it provides a network of friends who can assist with errands, attend appointments, or simply share life's moments.

Divorce, widowhood, or life changes can leave you questioning where to live or how to afford it. House sharing can o er stability and a fresh start during these transitions.

At this stage, many women focus on personal growth and enjoying life. House sharing with like-minded individuals can enhance purpose and zest for life.

REASONS WHY HOUSE SHARING MAKES SENSE

Sharing Your Own Home:

- ♦ You have unused rooms and space.
- ♦ Maintaining your home alone is financially and physically draining.
- ♦ You've decluttered and are willing to make renovations.

Sharing Someone Else's Home:

- ♦ Financial stress makes house sharing a practical option.
- ♦ You're ready for a new communal lifestyle.
- ♦ You value the companionship, financial relief, and sense of community house sharing offers.

TOP 10 ESSENTIAL DESIGN TIPS TO MAKE YOUR HOME ROOMMATE-READY

1. Divide Common Areas Into Zones
2. Create Semi-Private Spaces
3. Maximize Storage

4. Design Multi-Functional Suites
5. Optimize Other Bedrooms
6. Renovate Bathrooms With Universal Design
7. Upgrade the Kitchen
8. Utilize Nooks
9. Create a Communication Center
10. Enhance Outdoor Spaces

GOLDEN GIRLS LIFESTYLE REVISITED

The idea of house sharing might remind you of the Golden Girls TV series, where roommates from different walks of life shared a home and created lifelong bonds. Today, house sharing can offer similar benefits: financial freedom, companionship, and a supportive community, helping you thrive in your golden years.

Lifestyle Design (Minimalist's Mindset)

JOURNAL PROMPTS

- ♦ Overcome resistance:
- ♦ What fears or hesitations do you have about sharing your home? How could you address or reframe them?
- ♦ Your ideal roommate:
- ♦ Describe the traits of a roommate you'd love to live with. What shared values or interests would make for a great connection?

Quick Exercise
Golden Girls Vision Map

- ♦ Set a timer for 5 minutes and imagine your ideal house-sharing scenario.
- ♦ Quickly sketch or list what your shared space would look and feel like (e.g., cheerful kitchen, cozy common areas, supportive energy).
- ♦ Circle one element that feels most exciting or achievable to you.
- ♦ Think of one immediate step to bring that element to life.

Quick Tips

- ♦ Picture Your Roommate(s): See yourself interacting positively, laughing, and supporting each other.
- ♦ Feel the Benefits: Focus on how the financial relief, companionship, and shared responsibilities feel.
- ♦ Write a Goal: Open your eyes and jot down one small step you can take today to move toward house sharing.

NOTES:
_____
_____
_____

Confronting our self-limiting beliefs is one of the best gifts we can give ourselves.

Often, the "stories" we tell ourselves are outdated and need an upgrade.

Lifestyle Design (Minimalist's Mindset)

ARTICLE 5

Silver Learnings: How Covid-19 Turned Out to Be the Best Thing That Happened to Me

REPORT CARD DAY

Remember report card day? The handwritten notes from teachers, academic grades, effort grades, even "deportment" grades.

At our house, it was a family ritual. Sitting around the kitchen table, Mom would serve one of her favorite casseroles. After our lively conversations about the day, Dad would inevitably say, "Let's have a look at your report cards."

For me, that phrase brought dread—not because of my grades, which were a mix of B's, C's, and the occasional A, but because my sisters consistently excelled.

One by one, we handed over our report cards. Dad always showed genuine interest, acknowledging our achievements and asking how we might improve where we struggled.

CONVERSATIONS THAT CHANGE LIVES

While Dad never compared us, I couldn't help but feel less capable than my sisters. Yet, a life-changing moment happened years later, unrelated to those report cards.

As a high school freshman, my guidance counselor reviewed my PSAT results and said, "You're probably not college material and should pursue another path."

That single comment ignited a fire in me. I became determined to thrive—not just in college, but in life.

Our middle-class parents worked tirelessly to save for our education. Mom used a cash envelope budget system, visually dedicating funds for food, the mortgage, and college for her five children.

How dare that guidance counselor suggest I wasn't college material!

That afternoon, I told Mom what had happened. Without hesitation, she grabbed my arm, drove me back to school, and stormed into the counselor's office.

"How dare you tell my daughter she's not college material? We've saved for all of our children to go to college. She will go—and she will excel!"

Inspiration to Defy Expectations

Mom's passionate defense of me became a touchstone throughout my life. Whenever doubts crept in, I remembered her fierce belief in my potential.

For the past 35 years, I've owned a successful interior design firm, completing projects from Supreme Court Justice chambers to tiny houses. I found my niche, focusing on areas where I naturally excel.

But like many, I avoided areas where I lacked confidence, relying on others for tasks that didn't come easily— particularly anything related to technology.

A New Challenge: Learning What I Once Avoided

Then Covid-19 changed everything. Overnight, I had to shutter my business and adapt to working from home. Tasks I had delegated for years were now mine to figure out.

The pandemic pushed me to learn what I had long resisted.

- ♦ I retrained my brain to say, "I can" instead of "I can't."
- ♦ I proved to myself that I could embrace new skills and thrive.

Lifestyle Design (Minimalist's Mindset)

Reframing the Stories We Tell Ourselves

I share this deeply personal story because many Baby Boomers face similar challenges. We've told ourselves for years:

> "I'm not good with technology."

> "I don't know how."

> "I'll have someone else do it for me."

Covid-19 forced us to confront these outdated beliefs. It taught us to say, "I don't know how—yet. But I'm willing to learn."

A Brave New World (and a Brave New You)

Recently, I delivered a keynote address via Zoom to over 1,000 people—a speech I would have once given on stage. Though initially daunted, I embraced the challenge and succeeded.

It took a pandemic to push me out of my comfort zone and see what was possible.

What about you? Have you crashed through your self-limiting beliefs and accomplished something new? Share your story and let's grow together.

JOURNAL PROMPTS

- ♦ What limiting belief have you overcome in the past year? What helped you push through?
- ♦ Write about a time someone believed in you more than you believed in yourself. How did it impact you?
- ♦ What is one thing you've been avoiding learning or doing? How could mastering it change your life?

Quick Exercise

- ♦ Brainstorm Breakthrough: Take a blank sheet of paper. Write down one fear or challenge. In 2 minutes, jot down as many possible solutions as you can. Use the remaining 3 minutes to choose one and commit to action.

Quick Tips

- ♦ Reframe Negativity: When faced with "I can't," add the word "yet" to the end of the sentence.
- ♦ Start Small: Pick one new skill or habit to tackle and dedicate just 5 minutes a day to it.
- ♦ Celebrate Progress: Acknowledge every step forward, no matter how small—it builds momentum.

NOTES:

_____
_____
_____
_____
_____

CHAPTER V

Adventure and Financial Freedom—Freedom Through Minimalism

Have you been wondering, Whatever happened to the "old" me? The one who was fearless, fun, and free?

It might be time to give yourself a reboot—or a good old-fashioned kick in the pants.

ARTICLE 1

Bring Back the Adventure, Freedom, and Fun That's Been Missing from Your Life!

Have you noticed that your spirit of adventure has faded? Do you no longer wake up excited to tackle your day? What happened to the brave, bold, and spontaneous woman you used to be?

You know the one: passionate about life, fearless, and unwilling to let anything stand in her way of living fully each day.

She was confident, believed in herself, and embraced risks.
She was never too tired or too busy to try something new.
She always said *yes* to life.
She was unstoppable.

Is that woman gone forever, or is she just stuck—waiting for a reboot or perhaps a big kick in the pants? Has she settled for the "status quo"? Has she abandoned her dreams of adventure, freedom, and fun?

Or can that fiery spirit be reignited once again?

DO YOU FEEL STUCK?

You're not alone. Many women feel trapped—by life, work, or even their own routines. Maybe you're stuck in a job or career that's going nowhere. Maybe your relationship has lost its spark, or you're navigating life alone after a divorce or the loss of a spouse.

Perhaps you're an empty nester or recently retired, unsure of what the next chapter holds. Or maybe you're simply feeling the effects of aging.

Adventure and Financial Freedom—Freedom Through Minimalism

Whatever the cause, being stuck can feel overwhelming. But the good news is, you don't have to stay there.

TAKE A CLOSER LOOK AT YOUR LIFE

Be honest with yourself:

- Are you just going through the motions without passion or purpose?
- Are you waking up to the same old "status quo" life every day?
- Are you pretending everything's fine when, deep down, you know it's not?
- Are you ignoring your desire to live life more fully?
- Are you standing in your own way, blocking the path to your dreams?

WHAT'S STOPPING YOU?

It takes courage to admit that you've lost sight of your dreams. But acknowledging this is the first step to reigniting that passion and reclaiming your sense of adventure.

Believe it or not, a few simple changes can:

- Wake you up and shake you up.
- Help you break free from your comfort zone.
- Inspire you to take chances and believe in yourself again.
- Reboot, recharge, and reignite your life.

So, let's explore ten steps to bring back adventure, freedom, and fun into your life!

10 STEPS TO REDISCOVER ADVENTURE, FREEDOM, AND FUN

1. Create a Vision for Your Life One Year from Now

Ask yourself:

- What's most important to you?
- What have you done in the past that you'd like to rediscover?
- What new experiences do you want to explore—places, people, or challenges?
- What scares you but excites you at the same time?

Commit to this vision. Remember, life is a choice. Without action, nothing happens.

2. Adopt a Vacation Mindset Every Day

- Be a tourist in your own town.
- Catch a sunrise or sunset.
- Stand in awe of nature—look up at the trees or gaze at the stars.
- Open yourself to the beauty and wonder around you.

3. Dare Yourself to Try Something New Every Day

Surprise even yourself by breaking out of your routine. For inspiration, read *I Dare Me* by Lu Ann Cahn, who transformed her life by doing something new every day for a year.

Whether it's trying stand-up comedy, zip-lining, or dyeing your hair pink—just go for it!

4. See Life Through a New Lens

Shift your perspective. Rediscover child-like wonder and excitement. Practice mindfulness and learn to see the ordinary as extraordinary.

5. Let Go of Old Habits and Negative Thinking

Challenge yourself to adopt a positive mindset. Let go of self-doubt and habits that no longer serve you. Take back control of your life.

6. Tune Out to Tune In

Focus on what truly matters. Remove distractions, negativity, and toxic influences from your life. Surround yourself with people who uplift you.

7. Declutter Your Home and Mind

Simplify your life by letting go of the "stuff" that's weighing you down. Make room for the life you want by removing what no longer serves you.

8. Learn Something New

Step outside your comfort zone and tackle your fears. Take a class, pick up a new hobby, or finally start that side hustle you've been dreaming about.

9. Say YES to Life

Stop making excuses. Say yes to new experiences, invitations, and people. Reconnect with child-like joy by embracing playfulness—roll down a hill, have a water balloon fight, or dance in the rain.

10. Think Like a Champion

Doubts are normal, but don't let them define you. Use them as fuel to challenge yourself and strive for more.

Designing and living the life you truly want isn't always easy, but it's worth it. Don't wait—start today.

FINAL THOUGHTS

What would you do if you could get unstuck? What dreams are you still holding onto?

Rita Wilkins, "The Downsizing Designer"

Don't let fear or complacency hold you back. Take that first step toward living the life you deserve—a life full of adventure, freedom, and fun.

So, what's stopping you?

Adventure and Financial Freedom—Freedom Through Minimalism

JOURNAL PROMPTS

- ♦ Values Discovery: List five moments when you felt truly happy or fulfilled. What values were being honored in those moments?
- ♦ Time Audit: Write down how you spend a typical day. Highlight activities that drain you and circle ones that energize you.
- ♦ Personal Legacy: Imagine it's 10 years from now. What do you want people to say about how you lived your life?

Quick Exercise

Gratitude Inventory: Write down three things you're grateful for in your life right now. Then list three things you'd like to improve and why.

Quick Tips

- ♦ Batch Small Wins: Identify one area of your life that feels chaotic (e.g., your calendar or workspace). Dedicate 30 minutes to simplifying it and enjoy the immediate sense of control.
- ♦ Reframe Fear: When you catch yourself feeling afraid of change, ask, "What's the best thing that could happen if I take this leap?" Write down your answer to shift from fear to possibility.
- ♦ Connect Your Why: Before committing to any task or responsibility, ask yourself, "Does this align with my long-term goals and values?" Say no to what doesn't fit.

NOTES:

_____
_____
_____
_____
_____

Rita Wilkins, "The Downsizing Designer"

When your dreams become bigger than your fears, the impossible becomes possible—and eventually, inevitable. Give yourself permission to live your dreams starting today.

ARTICLE 2

10 Lessons That Come From Living Outside of Your Comfort Zone

We all have dreams and bucket lists that we would like to accomplish in our lifetime. Seeing that most of us are past 60, we have likely completed many of them. Yet, there may still be a few important items that continue to be relegated to our "someday" list. As the book title by Sam Horn states, *Someday Is Not a Day in the Week*.

Why do we continue to push those important dreams to the bottom of our "To-Do" list? Shouldn't they be at the top? After all, as baby boomer women in our Third Act, isn't this our time to finally make room for what matters most to us?

Last November, as I was writing my book, *Downsize Your Life, Upgrade Your Lifestyle: Secrets to More Time, Money and Freedom*, I was stopped dead in my tracks as I posed this question:

> "What is preventing you from having the kind of life you dream of right now?"

A RENEWED SENSE OF URGENCY

Right now. Those words shook me to my core and at the same time created a new sense of urgency. For years, my number one bucket list dream had been to immerse myself in the countryside of Southern France for at least 30 days.

I wanted to live like a local, experience their lifestyle, culture—and yes, their food—as if I were one of them. And while I was there, I also wanted to test our new lifestyle business model, Work 3 Days, Play 4, which balances having a great business and a great life.

I suddenly realized that I had not given myself permission to live out my big dream and fully live the life I most wanted. I began to wonder "what if":

- I took that 30-day journey to the South of France and prototyped our new *Work 3, Play 4* business model?
- I made my dream my reality? Not someday but one day soon.
- I didn't go? And yes, the thought did cross my mind.

It opened my eyes to a whole new way of living that I wanted not just for myself but also for other baby boomer women. My mantra became, "If not now, when?" I decided I was not going to live a life of regret.

What once seemed like an impossible dream became possible, then inevitable. I didn't know how I would do it, but my dream became larger than my fears. Nothing would stop me now that I had finally given myself permission to boldly and unapologetically live the life of my dreams.

On July 1, 2019, I landed in Marseille, France, beginning a journey that changed my life.

Let me share the lessons I learned from living out of my comfort zone for 30 days.

HAVING NO PLAN WAS THE BEST PLAN (FOR ME)

If I was going to experience the French countryside, culture, and people the way that I truly wanted, I decided the best way for me was to have no plan that might prevent me from having the freedom, flexibility, and spontaneity I wanted.

So, I only had a ticket to, a ticket from, a hotel reservation for my first night, and a small carry-on suitcase. Traveling with no itinerary was frightening but provided freedom I had never experienced before.

The most interesting result of traveling without a plan was that it invited a spirit of adventure that made me feel fully alive, 20 years younger, and authentically connected to the woman I've always wanted to be.

EXPECT THE UNEXPECTED: STUFF HAPPENS!

The bed and breakfast that I accidentally booked in the middle of nowhere.

The hotel reservation that didn't exist because I forgot to push send.

The bus that never arrived, leaving me stranded 50 kilometers from anything.

These are just a few of the "oops" moments that actually became part of the fun. "Figuring it out" became a finely-honed skill set. Getting lost, having no internet access, or taxi service simply provided many opportunities to grow, learn, and laugh at myself.

EMBRACE LIFE ON THE SKINNY BRANCHES

As a lifetime entrepreneur, I have taken many risks and thought I had become accustomed to being out of my comfort zone.

However, as a baby boomer woman who is directionally and tech-challenged, traveling to a country where everything was new clearly tested my ability to figure things out. The bigger the challenge, the more resilient I became.

YES, YOU WILL GET LONELY (SOMETIMES)

I had decided to travel solo, and because I've traveled alone many times before, I fully expected that I would occasionally get lonely… and I did. But I also discovered a few powerful ways to deal with loneliness:

- ♦ Acknowledge your feelings, write them down. Pray. Talk to loved ones back home.
- ♦ Push yourself to get out and engage with people. I found that the village squares were my favorite go-to places to meet new friends and socialize with locals.

- Take selfies, videos, and record experiences in your journal. It's important to capture those moments so that you can recall the memories and share them later.

It takes courage to travel alone, and while it has its downfalls, it certainly has its many benefits too. You get to do what you want, when you want, where you want—and you get to do it your way!

SEE MORE OF LESS

Could I have seen the entire country in 30 days? Probably, but my dream was to immerse myself in the French countryside so I could have a deeper experience.

- Slow down. Savor more.
- Focus on what interests you most.
- Take time to notice the little things.
- Do it in your own time and on your own terms.

ATTITUDE OR MINDSET CAN MAKE OR BREAK YOUR JOURNEY

To say this trip was easy would be a lie. I had to accept delays, develop patience, embrace challenges, and face my fears many times. I could have let several moments ruin my trip, but I chose to have a positive mindset regardless of circumstances.

- Have fun each day. Laugh at yourself, your missteps, and not knowing.
- Turn fear into curiosity and curiosity into fun.
- Learn to accept help from others. Just because you can do it yourself doesn't mean you have to.
- Have an open mind. Let go of preconceived ideas and judgments.

THE SIGNIFICANCE OF IMMERSIVE OR EXPERIENTIAL TRAVEL

Everyone and everything is a teacher. It's an opportunity to listen, learn, connect, and honor those things that are different from what we know. Being friendly and curious with locals allowed me to develop new friendships (which I'm still nurturing today).

This immersive travel experience created valuable conversations and insights that enriched my worldview to understand new points of view and new ways of living.

- ♦ Priceless experiences, rich conversations, and lifelong new friends.
- ♦ A newfound awareness and respect for our similarities and differences.
- ♦ A broader understanding and connection to the world around us.

SEIZE THE OPPORTUNITY TO SEE YOURSELF THROUGH A NEW LENS

Several years ago, when I downsized from a very large home to my tiny jewel-box apartment, I discovered the real me who had been hiding under all of my stuff.

Similarly, when I immersed myself in the South of France for 30 days, I discovered a new me that had been waiting to be found.

- ♦ I discovered the bold, fearless adventurer who thrives on change, challenge, and connection.
- ♦ I discovered that it is possible to have a great lifestyle and a great business working from anywhere in the world.
- ♦ I discovered saying yes to my dreams is one of the best decisions I have ever made.

EMBRACE A VACATION MINDSET EVERY DAY FOR THE REST OF YOUR LIFE

When we are on vacation, we are more relaxed, free, curious, and open to new ideas, people, and places. I discovered that we don't need to be on vacation to have a vacation mindset.

We simply need to open our eyes to adventure and opportunities that are right in front of us so that we can be fully alive each day. Living expectantly, daring ourselves to try new things, is all part of what makes life worthwhile. There's no need to wait for your next vacation. Live it now.

IT IS POSSIBLE TO DESIGN AND LIVE A LIFE YOU LOVE

At this stage in our lives, we have already accomplished much that we are proud of. And yet, we might still find ourselves asking, "What else can I do to be more and to do more?"

My 30-day journey provided the much-needed time to discern what matters most to me and where I can make the biggest impact during my Third Act. It's never too late to reimagine, reinvent, and redesign our lives.

WHERE I AM NOW

As baby boomer women in our Third Act, it is our time to follow those dreams, to check o those bucket list items before it's too late. It's important to see through the invisible barriers, both real and imagined, that prevent us from living the life we most want.

Whether your dream is to travel to distant locations, start a new business, or move closer to your grandchildren, give yourself permission to say "yes" to the life you want. Get comfortable with stepping out of your comfort zone and connect with the inner you that is desperately waiting to be found.

Adventure and Financial Freedom—Freedom Through Minimalism

JOURNAL PROMPTS

- When was the last time you stepped outside your comfort zone?
- How did it feel to take that leap, and what did you learn from it?
- What's one fear you can face this week to stretch yourself further?

Quick Exercise

The 10-Minute Decluttering Sprint

- Set a timer for 10 minutes.
- Choose one small area (a drawer, a shelf, or your bedside table).
- Quickly go through the items and ask yourself: *Do I use this? Does it bring me joy?*
- Set aside items you no longer need for donation or disposal.
- Celebrate your progress—it's a step toward a clutter-free life!

Quick Tips

- **Start Small and Stay Focused**

  Pick one small area, like a single drawer, and focus on that. Avoid the temptation to tackle too much at once.

- **Create a "Joy or No" Box**

  Place items in a box and revisit it after a week. If you haven't missed or thought about them, it's a sign they can be let go.

- **Set a "One In, One Out" Rule**

  For every new item you bring into your home, commit to removing one item. This keeps clutter in check while encouraging intentionality.

Rita Wilkins, "The Downsizing Designer"

NOTES:

Adventure and Financial Freedom—Freedom Through Minimalism

Online shopping is convenient and has simplified our lives, but it often encourages us to spend more than we plan or budget. Buyer beware!

Rita Wilkins, "The Downsizing Designer"

ARTICLE 3

Stop Wasting Money! 5 Effective Strategies to Reduce the Temptation to Overbuy Online

Do you find yourself mindlessly shopping online? If so, you're not alone. This has become a growing concern for consumers of all ages.

AN INTERESTING STATISTIC

The average American consumer spends over $1,000 per year on impulse online purchases, making at least six impulse buys per month.

Online shopping has become an integral part of our daily lives across all generations. With just a few clicks, you can have almost anything you want or need delivered to your door the next day.

No wonder this huge temptation has led to online shopping becoming such a prevalent issue in this digital age.

WHY IS IT SO HARD TO RESIST THE ALLURE OF EXCESSIVE ONLINE SHOPPING?

Easy Access

The truth is, the convenience and easy access of online shopping can be a slippery slope that comes with a cost. At any time of day or night, one click can lead to another and then another. Before you know it, you've spent more money than you intended. This leads not just to overspending, but also to overbuying and an accumulation of unnecessary items.

As fun as it might be to see an Amazon package on your doorstep, the constant influx of packages can also lead to guilt, buyer's remorse, and even marital disputes.

Adventure and Financial Freedom—Freedom Through Minimalism

Emotional Triggers

Impulse online shopping is frequently triggered by our emotions:

- **Fear of missing out** on a good deal
- **Boredom, loneliness, anger, or stress**
- **Social influence** or the desire to fit in

It's easy to get triggered when mindlessly shopping on the internet and social media. In a weak moment, you click "buy now."

Targeted Ads

Targeted ads are another major culprit when it comes to online shopping temptation. Advertisers use sophisticated algorithms to target our specific interests and demographics, encouraging us to click the "buy now" button.

To make matters worse, social media influencers and celebrities often promote products, making us feel like we need to have them, too.

EFFECTIVE STRATEGIES TO OVERCOME ONLINE IMPULSE BUYING

1. Set a Budget

The first critical step to combat online shopping temptation is to set a budget and stick to it. When you're mindful of how much you can spend, you're more likely to make conscious purchasing decisions.

2. Track Your Spending

Use apps like **Mint** or **Personal Capital** to track spending and stay on top of your finances. These easy-to-use tools will help you monitor your habits and stay accountable.

3. Emotional Awareness

Recognize and acknowledge your emotional triggers. Are you mindlessly shopping online because you're stressed, bored, or lonely? Identifying these patterns can help you address the underlying issues, allowing you to find healthier coping mechanisms such as exercise or journaling.

4. Use Online Tools

Install browser extensions like **uBlock Origin** or **News Feed Eradicator**. These tools help block targeted ads, making it less likely for you to be tempted.

5. Practice Intentional Spending

One of the most powerful tools to overcome online shopping urges is the satisfaction you feel when you save money by being mindful about what you're purchasing and how much you're spending.

It feels great to know you are in control, resisting temptation, and making conscious decisions to spend your money wisely.

TAKE BACK CONTROL OF YOUR ONLINE SPENDING

Overcoming online shopping temptation requires awareness, intentionality, and strategy. By acknowledging emotional triggers, setting a budget, and using apps to track your spending, you can regain control over your online shopping habits.

Adventure and Financial Freedom—Freedom Through Minimalism

JOURNAL PROMPTS

- ♦ Reflect on a time when you resisted the urge to buy something online.
- ♦ How did it feel? What helped you overcome the temptation?
- ♦ Write about the emotions and confidence you experienced by staying in control.

Quick Exercise

- ♦ Next time you feel the urge to shop impulsively, stop and take three deep breaths.
- ♦ Then, write down the item and why you want it.
- ♦ Wait 24 hours before deciding whether to purchase it. Often, the desire will pass.

Quick Tips

- ♦ **Implement a 30-Day Rule**: For non-essential items, add them to a wish list and wait 30 days before purchasing. You'll often find you don't need them after all.
- ♦ **Designate a Shopping Day:** Limit online shopping to one day per week or month. This helps create boundaries and encourages thoughtful purchases.

NOTES:

_____
_____
_____
_____
_____

While teaching kids about money matters, good money habits don't just happen. When you start teaching your kids and grandkids about money early on and when you lead by good example, you're giving them a gift that they will treasure for a lifetime.

ARTICLE 4

Why Teaching Grandkids About Money Early Matters

Did you know that only 17% of high school students are required to take a personal finance course? Unfortunately, many of us didn't learn much about personal finance or investing at home or in school during our formative years.

THE GIFT OF FINANCIAL EDUCATION: MONEY SKILLS AND FINANCIAL FREEDOM

Teaching grandkids about money is crucial because money is an integral part of daily life. Planting these seeds early is essential, even while they're still riding scooters, swinging on monkey bars, or coloring with crayons.

Introducing children to concepts like earning, saving, spending, and managing money wisely helps them understand the value of a dollar. These lessons shape good money habits and smart financial decisions as they grow.

By instilling positive habits, we teach financial responsibility, build confidence, and encourage better decision-making. These skills help prevent common financial pitfalls, such as credit card debt, living without a budget, and struggling to manage money.

WHY PARENTS AND GRANDPARENTS SHOULD TEACH KIDS ABOUT MONEY

Too often, parents avoid teaching their kids about money, thinking they're too young to understand. Others assume their children will learn financial management skills later in life.

This is a mistake. Left to figure out money on their own, kids may pick up both good and bad habits from friends, social media, or trial and error. They also observe their parents' financial behaviors, sometimes unknowingly adopting poor habits that can lead to financial stress, paycheck-to-paycheck living, or debt.

Breaking this cycle starts with teaching kids good money habits early. This is where grandparents can play a vital role. With your life experience, you know the good, the bad, and the ugly of managing—or mismanaging—money.

Teaching Kids About Money Is Simple

Teaching kids about money doesn't have to be complicated. Keep it simple, practical, interactive, and fun!

Use age-appropriate methods, real-life examples, and hands-on activities to engage them. The key is to start early, stay consistent, and make learning enjoyable.

AGE-APPROPRIATE MONEY LESSONS

Ages 3 to 7

- **Piggy Bank and Play Money:**

    Introduce young children to coins and the concept that money has value. Encourage saving by using a piggy bank and let them see how money adds up over time.

- **Play Store:**

    Use a pretend store setting to teach kids about making choices, purchases, and basic counting.

Adventure and Financial Freedom—Freedom Through Minimalism

Ages 8 to 12

- **Earning an Allowance:**

    Allow kids to earn a regular allowance by doing chores. This teaches earning, budgeting, saving, and responsible spending while encouraging goal-setting.

- **Grocery Shopping Game:**

    Give them a small budget and let them make decisions within it. They'll learn about prioritizing needs and wants—and occasionally experience the consequences of poor choices.

Ages 13 to 18

- **Savings Accounts and Compound Interest:**

    Introduce them to savings accounts and explain how compound interest works. If they use a debit card, link it to their savings account to encourage responsibility.

- **Family Financial Discussions:**

    Involve teens in discussions about household expenses like rent, utilities, and groceries. This teaches them the real costs of living.

Ages 18 and Beyond

- **Credit and Loans:** Explain how credit and loans work, including student loans, car loans, and mortgages. Emphasize the importance of maintaining a good credit score and understanding compounding interest when saving or borrowing.

FUN FAMILY ACTIVITIES TO TEACH KIDS ABOUT MONEY

- **Entrepreneurship:**
  Encourage activities like a lemonade stand or selling crafts. This introduces concepts of earning, expenses, and profits.

- **Board Games:**
  Games like *Monopoly* teach buying, selling, and investing principles in an entertaining way.

- **Grocery Shopping:**
  Teach decision-making, price comparison, budgeting, and the value of coupons during routine shopping trips.

HOW TO RAISE GRATEFUL, RESPECTFUL, RESPONSIBLE, AND NON-ENTITLED KIDS

This is one of the biggest challenges parents and grandparents face today. While some "good spoiling" is okay— especially from grandparents—too much can overwhelm children and lead to unintended consequences.

Excessive toys, gadgets, or clothes can overstimulate kids, reduce focus, and diminish creativity. Simplifying their environment helps children thrive. Less truly is more.

Finding Balance

While it's important to provide for your children, avoid overindulging them to the point they don't appreciate their possessions. Striking the right balance is essential for raising grateful, not entitled, kids.

- **Set Limits and Stick to Them:**
  Say "no" often—and mean it. Teach the value of delayed gratification.

Adventure and Financial Freedom—Freedom Through Minimalism

- **Buy Fewer Things:**

    Spend more time creating meaningful experiences with your kids rather than buying material things.

Teaching kids about money from an early age lays the foundation for lifelong financial success. By fostering responsibility, instilling good habits, and making financial lessons fun, you equip your grandchildren with the skills they need to make smart money decisions for years to come.

JOURNAL PROMPTS

- **Money Memories:**

  Write about your earliest memory involving money. What emotions or lessons were tied to that experience?

- **Planning a Fun Money Activity:**

  How can you creatively teach a financial concept to your grandkids in a way that's both practical and enjoyable?

- **Assessing Your Money Habits:**

  How do your current money habits set an example for younger generations? Are there areas you'd like to improve?

Quick Exercise

Mini Shopping Game

1. **Set Up a Play Store:** Gather a few items like a diaper, a toy, a snack, or a book and assign each a price using small sticky notes.
2. **Give Them Play Money:** Hand out a few coins or dollar bills (real or play money).
3. **Shop for Needs First:** Explain they need to buy important items (like diapers or snacks) before they can use money for "wants" like toys.
4. **Let Them Shop:** Watch as they choose items, encouraging them to think about what they *need* versus what they *want*.

Quick Tips

- **Start With Storytelling:**

  Share simple, relateable stories from your own life about financial successes and mistakes. Kids love hearing personal anecdotes, and it makes the lessons stick.

Adventure and Financial Freedom—Freedom Through Minimalism

- ♦ **Lead by Example:**
  Be mindful of how you talk about money around children. Use positive language, demonstrate budgeting, and show gratitude for what you have.

NOTES:

Rita Wilkins, "The Downsizing Designer"

There is comfort in owning less. Decorating for the holidays is no longer a time-consuming chore. Rather, it becomes a chance to focus on simply enjoying the true essence and meaning of the holiday season.

ARTICLE 5

Downsized? How to Decorate Your New Smaller Home for the Holidays

At this stage of life, you're looking forward to a simpler lifestyle with less clutter, more freedom, new friends, and new memories.

Your kids are now grown and have left the nest. You might be single, widowed, or a couple. No matter what, holidays have changed for you. The once bustling household filled with your children, family, and friends is suddenly quieter… especially if they won't be coming home for the holidays this year.

A welcome respite from the overwhelm and stress of past holiday seasons, but also a little unnerving because you don't know how to make your smaller home feel like Christmas!

DECORATING BACK THEN

Do you remember all those years you went "all out" to decorate every inch of your large home to make it look and feel like a Christmas Wonderland?

You'd spend weeks preparing—decorating, pulling boxes up from the basement full of stored holiday decorations to create the magic of a Hallmark Christmas.

Just when you thought you were finished and could relax, you'd find one more area that needed decorating! Everything had to be just perfect. And as soon as that was done, something else would get in the way of you slowing down long enough to simply enjoy what you had created.

But now that you've decluttered and downsized, you have less stuff and less space.

Rita Wilkins, "The Downsizing Designer"

Life just got a little easier when it comes to decorating for the holidays. Downsizing has given you an opportunity to rethink overdecorating. It has also allowed you to "change things up" and do things differently by intentionally creating new traditions with new friends while savoring only the old traditions that matter most to you.

8 TIPS FOR DECORATING YOUR NEW SMALLER HOME FOR THE HOLIDAYS

As the "Downsizing Designer" and a nationally recognized interior designer for over 35 years, these are my top 8 tips for decorating your new smaller home so that it exudes the warmth and welcoming holiday feel that says, "Come sit a while. Let's just enjoy this beautiful holiday season together."

1. Create Your Vision and Goals for the New Holiday Look and Feel

Capture the simple essence of Christmas—a home that is warm, welcoming, and filled with traditional touches of holiday sounds, scents, color, and light.

This is your opportunity to design it exactly as you want: the feel, the look, the smells. Take the time upfront to intentionally create the environment that will be the backdrop for your wonderful holiday and the beginning of new traditions.

2. Decorate Your Smaller Home by Keeping It Simple

Less is more. When you think like a minimalist, you surround yourself only with things that have meaning and are beautiful to you.

Don't overdecorate. Use a few well-placed larger items for impact, avoiding too many small items that can look cluttered, especially in a small space.

3. Immerse Yourself in the Experience of Decorating

With fewer rooms to decorate and a pared-down collection of holiday decor, decorating no longer feels like a chore.

Embrace the process: pick a day, set out your decorations, turn on your favorite holiday music, light some candles, and pour a fine glass of wine. Make it a memorable and enjoyable experience.

4. Be Creative with What You Already Have

You'll soon realize you probably have everything you need right in front of you. Instead of buying more, look around your home and get creative with what you already own. See your decorations with fresh eyes.

5. Be Inspired by Nature

Green is a healing color that brings life, balance, and peace. Be inspired by nature: green trees, wreaths, garlands, pinecones, and branches. Pair these with bold accents like red ribbons, poinsettias, and berries.

6. Experience the Magic of Lights

Lights create the magic. Use tree lights, candles, and accent lights to create a warm, inviting glow that beckons you to sit and savor the moment.

7. Decorate Early, Enjoy Longer

Once you're done decorating, stop! Be content with the ambiance you've created. Invite friends and family over to enjoy it too.

8. Create Special Moments

Now that the decorating is done, focus on creating new experiences and memories that will last a lifetime. Here are a few ideas:

Rita Wilkins, "The Downsizing Designer"

- **Santa's Give-Back Sack:** Teach your grandchildren to recycle their gently used toys by putting them into a Give-Back Sack for Santa to redistribute to other children.
- **Grandchildren's Tree:** Spend an afternoon making ornaments with your grandchildren to decorate a special tree. They can gift the handmade ornaments to their parents.
- **Lifetime Videos:** Share your holiday memories by recording interviews with your grandkids or creating videos with special holiday messages.
- **Try a New Recipe:** Use your extra time to prepare a favorite recipe or learn to create a new one.

As you relax and enjoy the beautiful new environment you designed, you'll discover that decluttering and downsizing have done more than make decorating simpler. They've given you the gift of time—time to embrace a new, simpler lifestyle and savor the true spirit of the season.

Adventure and Financial Freedom—Freedom Through Minimalism

JOURNAL PROMPTS
- What do I truly cherish about my holiday decorations? Reflect on which pieces bring the most joy and why.
- How can I create meaningful holiday traditions without relying on material items? Brainstorm non-material traditions that can replace excessive decor.

Quick Exercise
The 15-Minute Holiday Edit:
- Set a timer for 15 minutes.
- Gather all your holiday decorations in one place.
- Quickly sort into three categories:
  - **Keep:** Items you love and use yearly.
  - **Donate:** Items in good condition that no longer fit your style.
  - **Toss:** Broken or outdated items beyond repair.

Evaluate the "Keep" pile, ensuring it aligns with your current holiday vision.

QUICK TIPS
- **Embrace Multi-Functional Decor:** Choose items that work for multiple seasons, such as neutral string lights or greenery that transitions from fall to winter.
- **Create a Capsule Collection:** Limit decorations to one or two storage bins. This ensures you have enough to create a festive atmosphere without feeling overwhelmed.

Rita Wilkins, "The Downsizing Designer"

NOTES:

WATCH ON YOUTUBE:

SUPPLEMENTARY MATERIALS

Thank you for taking the time to review my new e-book. As a small token of appreciation, we have included three supplemental resources to further support your journey toward living an abundant life with less.

BONUS!

1. Decluttering Checklist
2. The Updated Reverse Bucket List
3. **BONUS ARTICLE:** The Secret of Living with Intention Starts with a Life Audit

Rita Wilkins, "The Downsizing Designer"

DECLUTTERING CHECKLIST

Minimalist Home Decluttering Checklist

Remove these 49 items from your HOME, and your LIFE
✓ UNUSED ✓ UNWANTED ✓ UNLOVED ✓ UNNECESSARY

YOUR HOME
1. Unused furniture
2. Unused clothing
3. Unused gifts
4. Unused decorative items
5. Unloved toys
6. Duplicates and multiples
7. Out of date food

YOUR TECH & ENTERTAINMENT
22. Unused gadgets
23. Unwatched videos
24. Unnecessary subscriptions
25. Unused apps
26. Outdated phones
27. Outdated CDs and DVDs
28. Excessive electronics

YOUR OFFICE
8. Unread books
9. Unread newspapers
10. Unused binders
11. Unused pens and pencils
12. Unnecessary paperwork
13. Unnecessary programs
14. Outdated receipts

YOUR CALENDAR
29. Unnecessary events
30. Unnecessary to-do list
31. Unnecessary routines
32. Overbooked schedule
33. Unnecessary multitasking
34. Unproductive habits
35. Unwanted apps

YOUR SOCIAL MEDIA:
15. Unnecessary memberships
16. Outdated contacts
17. Outdated emails
18. Unwanted notifications
19. Unfollow
20. Unfriend
21. Unplug

YOUR HEALTH & FITNESS:
36. Unused exercise equipment
37. Unused apps
38. Unhealthy foods
39. Unhealthy drinks
40. Unhealthy products
41. Unwanted stress
42. Unnecessary distractions

YOUR FINANCES:
43. Unnecessary debt
44. Unnecessary expenses
45. Unnecessary paper transactions
46. Unnecessary purchases
47. Unused apps
48. Unused services
49. Outdated files & receipts

By Rita Wilkins, The Downsizing Designer © Copyright Design Services LTD. - Privacy Policy

THE REVERSE BUCKET LIST

RECONNECT WITH YOUR DREAMS AND VISION FOR THE LIFE YOU REALLY WANT

WHY A REVERSE BUCKET LIST MATTERS: POWER OF PERSPECTIVE

A friend of mine recently lost her job due to a corporate downsizing. After the initial shock and a few weeks of anger and self-pity, she realized that being fired was actually a blessing in disguise.

She had been unhappy and dissatisfied with her job for a long time but stayed because it was comfortable. Looking back, she saw she had been going through the motions, disconnected, unfulfilled, and had lost sight of what truly mattered to her.

Getting let go became an opportunity to challenge herself, think differently, and explore a new, more meaningful direction for her career and life—one that would inspire her, bring satisfaction, and reignite her passion.

That's when I told her about the Reverse Bucket List—a powerful tool to shift focus from what she had yet to do to what she had already accomplished.

WHAT IS THE DIFFERENCE BETWEEN A TRADITIONAL AND A REVERSE BUCKET LIST?

Traditional Bucket List

A traditional bucket list is a list of things you hope to accomplish in the future. Examples:

- ❏ Run a marathon.
- ❏ Spend 3 months in Tuscany.
- ❏ Read 12 books every year.

It's a fun way to push yourself, try new things, and step out of your comfort zone. However, it can sometimes feel like an overwhelming to-do list, reminding you of all the things you haven't done yet.

THE REVERSE BUCKET LIST

REVERSE BUCKET LIST

A reverse bucket list, on the other hand, is about **reflecting on and celebrating the things you've already achieved**—big and small. It helps you cultivate gratitude, gain perspective, and recognize the experiences, lessons, and people who have shaped you.

By shifting your focus to accomplishments, you gain clarity about what truly matters and fuel your motivation for the future.

WHY CREATE A REVERSE BUCKET LIST?
The Benefits:

> **Gratitude**—Recognizing your past accomplishments fosters a deep appreciation for your journey.
>
> **Validation**—You develop newfound respect for your hard-earned lessons and achievements.
>
> **Clarity**—By identifying what brings you joy and fulfillment, you gain clarity on your values.
>
> **Motivation**—Rediscovering your purpose empowers you to move forward toward your dreams.
>
> **Vision & Roadmap**—Understanding what matters most helps you prioritize future goals.
>
> **Confidence**—Reflecting on past successes shifts your mindset and opens you up to new opportunities.
>
> **Perspective**—You realize you already have the tools to navigate future challenges.

5 ESSENTIAL STEPS TO CREATE YOUR OWN REVERSE BUCKET LIST

The Brain Dump

Set aside time to Reflect on and write down at least 50 things you've accomplished and are proud of. These can be personal, professional, or life experiences.

Categories to Consider:
- ❏ Goals you've achieved
- ❏ Milestones you've reached
- ❏ People who influenced you
- ❏ Places you've traveled
- ❏ Unique experiences
- ❏ Life-changing moments
- ❏ Relationships that shaped you
- ❏ Volunteer work
- ❏ Personal growth areas
- ❏ Skills you've learned
- ❏ Bold risks you took
- ❏ Other achievements

YOUR LIST:
- ❏ _____
- ❏ _____
- ❏ _____
- ❏ _____
- ❏ _____

THE REVERSE BUCKET LIST

- ❏ _____
- ❏ _____
- ❏ _____
- ❏ _____
- ❏ _____
- ❏ _____
- ❏ _____

TIME TO REFLECT

Take time to Reflect on your list and answer the following questions:

- ♦ What are you most proud of?
- ♦ What stood out the most and why?
- ♦ What experiences brought you the most joy and fulfillment?
- ♦ What lessons did you learn from your successes and failures?
- ♦ What obstacles did you overcome?
- ♦ What strengths did you tap into?

YOUR REFLECTIONS:

_____
_____
_____
_____
_____
_____
_____
_____

ACKNOWLEDGE YOURSELF

Recognizing your past accomplishments boosts confidence and self-awareness.

- How do you feel about what you've achieved?
- What are you most grateful for?
- What insights have you gained from this Reflection?
- How has this exercise inspired or impacted you?
- Do you feel more connected to what truly matters to you?

YOUR THOUGHTS:

THE REVERSE BUCKET LIST

YOUR NEW VISION & ROADMAP

Now that you have clarity on your past accomplishments, create a vision for the future that aligns with what matters most.

- What do you want more of in your life? Less of?
- What goals align with your passions and purpose?
- What steps will you take to make them happen?
- Create a timeline for prioritizing these goals.

YOUR VISION & ROADMAP:

_____
_____
_____
_____
_____
_____
_____
_____
_____

ONGOING UPDATES

Your reverse bucket list is a living document. Revisit it often to:

- Add new accomplishments
- Reflect on lessons learned
- Continue acknowledging yourself
- Expand your vision for the life you truly want

FINAL SECTION: TAKING ACTION & STAYING INSPIRED

Next Steps Challenge:
- ♦ Share one accomplishment from your list with a friend or loved one.
- ♦ Set a reminder to revisit this list in 6 months and add new achievements.
- ♦ Create a small vision board or collage with highlights from your list.
- ♦ Journal about how your past wins have shaped your present and future.

Taking action reinforces your achievements and helps you move forward with clarity and purpose. Remember, **you've already accomplished so much—your next adventure awaits!**

FINAL THOUGHTS

Creating a reverse bucket list can have a profound impact on your life. It helps you realize that life is not just about checking o future goals—it's about appreciating the journey and celebrating how far you've already come.

Live each day with gratitude, passion, and no regrets.

#ReverseBucketList

#Gratitude

#MinimalistLiving

#PurposeDrivenLife

BONUS ARTICLE

Life Audit

THE SECRET OF LIVING WITH INTENTION STARTS WITH A LIFE AUDIT

Do you feel like you're drifting through life, caught up in the daily grind with no clear direction, no real purpose, and no true meaning?

Maybe you're feeling stuck, questioning whether this is the life you truly want. You might even find yourself asking, *What am I doing? Why am I doing this? Where am I going?*

Such was the case with a friend of mine. A highly successful business owner, she seemed to have it all, but when she reached out to me for coffee, I knew something must be wrong.

When she arrived, I barely recognized her. She looked exhausted, depleted, and overwhelmed. She mentioned that she had been watching my videos on living a simpler, more intentional life and wanted to know how to declutter her own life.

Her business was thriving, but she had no personal life beyond the office. Having just turned 60, she realized life was quickly passing her by. She was overwhelmed, stressed, unhappy, and desperate for work-life balance.

In her own words, her priorities were cluttered. She spent many years focused solely on growing her business, leaving little room for living her life.

In a moment of levity, I reminded her of a famous line from *Ferris Bueller's Day Off*: *"Life moves pretty fast. If you don't stop and look around once in a while, you could miss it!"*

My friend was lucky. She had a wake-up call. She realized she had a choice to intentionally create new priorities that would result in meaningful and lasting change… a new life filled with meaning, purpose, joy, and fun!

Whether it's a milestone birthday like my friend's, the beginning of a new year, a sudden "life quake", or a moment of quiet realization, we all face a time when we question if we're truly living the life we want.

If this resonates with you, a life audit could be the answer. It's not just about identifying what's wrong in your life, but also about acknowledging that you have the power to choose and the power to change.

A life audit helps you:

1. Reflect on where you are and where you want to go.
2. Reevaluate your priorities, goals, and habits.
3. Refocus on what matters and take action to align your life with your values, passions, and purpose.

WHAT IS A LIFE AUDIT AND WHY DOES IT MATTER?

A life audit is about ***you***—who you are, what you want, and what you need to live life to the fullest. It will help you uncover the hidden clutter that's preventing you from living the life you really want.

- ♦ It is a deep dive into your dreams, aspirations, goals, priorities, and habits.
- ♦ It helps you discover your passion and purpose so you can move forward with clarity, focus, and intention.
- ♦ It explores all areas of your life: career, relationships, finances, health, personal growth, spirituality, and fun.
- ♦ It is like a GPS because it shows you where you are, where you want to go, and what's holding you back.

Life Audit

Each step of the life audit works together like pieces of a puzzle. If you skip one, the picture remains incomplete. By taking time to complete all three essential steps, you'll gain clarity and confidence to design a life filled with purpose, meaning, balance, and joy.

THE 3 STEPS OF A LIFE AUDIT

A life audit consists of three essential steps:

1. **Vision Board:** Where do you want to go?
2. **Life Wheel:** Where are you now?
3. **Self-Reflection:** What matters most?

Each step builds on the others.

Skipping one is like trying to navigate without a map—you'll never reach your desired destination.

Step 1: Vision Board

See the future you want.

A vision board isn't just any old art project. It's a tool that helps you bring your goals to life. By visually presenting what you aspire to, you create a reminder of the life you want to build. A vision board should excite you because it helps you dream boldly while clarifying your passion and purpose and setting goals that truly matter to you.

Whether it's images of a peaceful home, a fulfilling career, or creating special moments with your loved ones, your vision board acts as a guiding light to help you stay focused on what matters most to you.

HOW TO CREATE A VISION BOARD

- ♦ Gather magazines, clip photos, sketches, and words or phrases that represent your dreams and goals.

- Create a collage that inspires you and Reflects the life you want to build.
- Place it somewhere visible to keep you motivated.

My Reflection on My Own Vision Board

When I created my first vision board, I realized how much energy I was wasting on things that didn't matter. Seeing my dreams visually represented gave me the clarity to focus on what truly matters.

Step 2: Life Wheel

Assess your present life.

Before you can map a route to your destination, you need to know your starting point.

The life wheel is a simple yet powerful tool that helps you evaluate key areas of your life: career, relationships, health, finances, spirituality, and more.

By ranking these areas, you can pinpoint where you feel fulfilled and where you need to grow. This clarity helps you prioritize your time, energy, and resources more effectively.

HOW TO CREATE A LIFE WHEEL

- Draw a circle or download a life wheel divided into sections representing different areas of your life.
- Color in each section to identify different areas.
- Rank each area on a scale from 1 to 10.
- Use the results to pinpoint where you're thriving and where you need to grow.

Life Audit

Your Life at a Glance

By Rita Wilkins
The Downsizing Designer

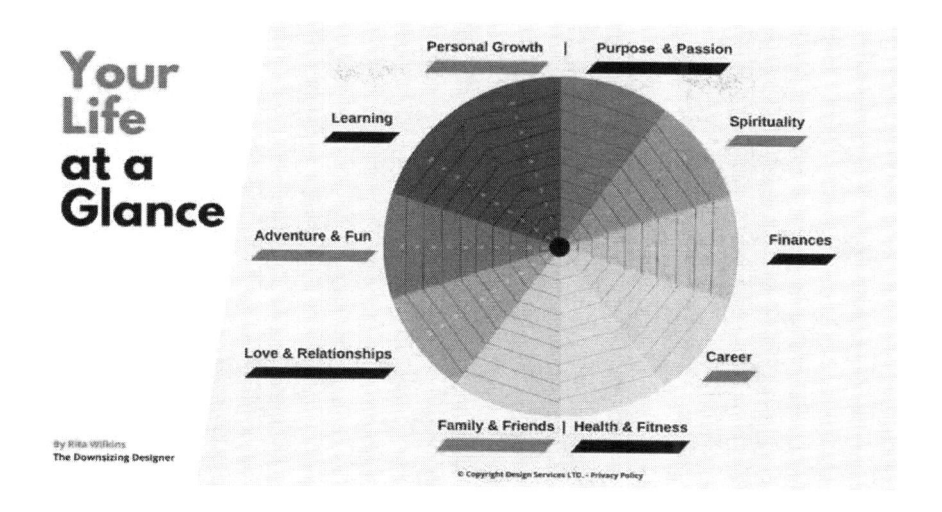

(Life wheel diagram with segments: Personal Growth | Purpose & Passion, Spirituality, Finances, Career, Health & Fitness, Family & Friends, Love & Relationships, Adventure & Fun, Learning)

© Copyright Design Services LTD. – Privacy Policy

My Reflection on My Life Wheel

When I used the life wheel, I quickly identified areas where I was out of balance and could more effectively focus my time and energy.

Step 3: Self-Reflection
Uncover what truly matters.

This is like your personal GPS. It helps uncover what drives you—your core values, your passions, and your purpose.

By Reflecting on and clearly articulating what lights you up, fills you up, and makes you truly happy and satisfied, life gets so much easier!

REFLECTION QUESTIONS:

1. What do you truly want from life, and are you moving in a direction that aligns with your passions and purpose?
2. What brings you the most joy and fulfillment, and how much time do you currently devote to it?

3. What are you most proud of, and what lessons have you learned from both successes and failures?
4. Who are the most important people in your life, and how do they contribute to your happiness and success?
5. What do you excel at and love doing? Are you incorporating these into your daily life?
6. What's missing from your life that would bring you greater fulfillment and align with your values?
7. What obstacles, internal or external, are holding you back?

My Reflections on Self-Reflection
One of my biggest breakthroughs was realizing how cluttered my priorities had been. By saying no to things that didn't align with my values, I created space for what truly mattered.

WHY ALL 3 STEPS MATTER
Each step of the life audit builds on the other:

- ♦ Without a vision board, you lack a clear destination.
- ♦ Without a life wheel, you can't assess the gaps between your dreams and reality.
- ♦ Without self-Reflection, you won't discover the deeper "why that makes you cry" behind meaningful goals.

Together, these steps provide clarity, focus, and motivation to create lasting change.

My Personal Insights

Living Simply, Intentionally, and Authentically

Perhaps the most significant insight I gained is the importance of living simply, intentionally, and authentically.

Life Audit

For many years, I tried to t into someone else's dream of a good life. I wasted time, money, and energy on trying to be something I wasn't... The big house, fancy cars, designer wardrobe.

When I began saying no to things that didn't align with my values and yes to only the people and things that brought me joy, meaning, and fulfillment, I discovered the real me that had been hiding beneath all those cluttered priorities.

I felt lighter, freer, and more peaceful. By following my personal GPS, I was finally in control of my own life. I discovered the real me.

THE POWER OF SUPPORTIVE RELATIONSHIPS

Another powerful insight I gained from my life audit is the importance of surrounding myself with people who truly care about me, support my goals, and encourage my aspirations.

Equally important is making sure they know that I will support them on their journeys as well.

By prioritizing simplicity, and living with less, my life has become richer, more abundant, and truly fulfilling. It made me realize how much more life I have to live and how much more I have to give!

Surrounding myself with supportive people enriched my life and allowed me to focus on what truly matters.

MEET RITA

YOUR LIFE MATTERS

I do hope you will take time for your own life audit so you can start living the life you truly want … and deserve.

A life audit is life-changing.

I invite you to invest your time and energy into completing your own life audit.

And if you will, please share your story, your wakeup call moments, your goals, and your insights.

Your story will make a difference to others.

WATCH NOW!
UNLOCK YOUR PURPOSE:
THE SECRET OF LIVING WITH INTENTION STARTS WITH
THIS 3-STEP LIFE AUDIT

THE DOWNSIZING DESIGNER

Rita Wilkins is a nationally recognized interior design and lifestyle design expert, a TEDx speaker, and author of the best-selling book, "Downsize Your Life, Upgrade Your Lifestyle: Secrets to More Time, Money, and Freedom." Also known as the "Downsizing Designer," Rita is committed to helping people learn how to declutter and downsize their lives so that they can live a simpler, more abundant life with less. As a minimalist herself, Rita is passionate about helping others experience the freedom of owning less by going from a life full of excess stuff to a life filled with meaning and purpose.

Learn More

https://www.designservicesltd.com/about/

PERSONAL MESSAGE TO MY READERS AND FOLLOWERS

Thank you for allowing me to use my voice and my God-given talents to share this curated collection of articles, interspersed with my own life-changing experiences on my journey to living a simpler life with less.

I truly hope they inspire, motivate, and empower you to experience the clarity, freedom, fulfillment, and joy that come when you let go of the things that stand in the way of the life you truly want.

Thank you for allowing me to be part of your journey. Whether you're just getting started, navigating the messy middle, or already enjoying a more abundant life with less, I hope you'll share your story with us—because we all learn from each other.

- Your story could be exactly what someone needs to hear right now.
- Your story could inspire someone to begin their own journey to less.
- Your story could be the encouragement someone needs to keep going.

Your story matters, so I hope you'll share what you've learned along the way—the good, the bad, and the ugly. By sharing your story and using your voice, you will impact people you may not even know. God bless you on your journey.

Rita J. Wilkins

Rita Wilkins "The Downsizing Designer"

Visit SHOP for more resources!
https://www.designservicesltd.com/store/

Made in the USA
Monee, IL
11 August 2025